The Commerce and Navigation of the Erythraean Sea

ANONYMI [ARRIANI UT FERTUR]

PERIPLUS MARIS ERYTHRÆI.

TRANSLATED FROM THE TEXT

As given in the *Geographi Græci Minores*, edited by
C. Muller : Paris, 1855.

WITH INTRODUCTION AND COMMENTARY.

THE

COMMERCE AND NAVIGATION

OF THE

ERYTHRÆAN SEA;

BEING A TRANSLATION

OF THE

PERIPLUS MARIS ERYTHRÆI,

BY AN ANONYMOUS WRITER,

AND OF

ARRIAN'S ACCOUNT OF THE VOYAGE OF NEARKHOS,

FROM THE MOUTH OF THE INDUS TO THE HEAD OF THE
PERSIAN GULF.

WITH INTRODUCTIONS, COMMENTARY, NOTES,
AND INDEX.

BY

J. W. McCRINDLE, M.A., Edin.,

PRINCIPAL OF THE GOVERNMENT COLLEGE, PATNA;
MEMBER OF THE COUNCIL OF THE UNIVERSITY OF EDINBURGH;
FELLOW OF THE CALCUTTA UNIVERSITY.

(Reprinted, with additions, from the Indian Antiquary.)

Calcutta:
THACKER, SPINK & Co.

Bombay:
ED. SOC. PRESS.

London:
TRÜBNER & Co.

1879.

BOMBAY :
PRINTED AT THE EDUCATION SOCIETY'S PRESS, BYCULLA.

PREFACE.

In the Preface to my former work, "Ancient India as described by Megasthenes and Arrian," I informed the reader that it was my intention to publish from time to time translations of the Greek and Latin works which relate to ancient India, until the series should be exhausted, and the present volume is the second instalment towards the fulfilment of that undertaking. It contains a translation of the *Periplûs* (i. e. *Circumnavigation*) of the *Erythræan Sea*, together with a translation of the second part of the *Indika* of Arrian describing the celebrated voyage made by Nearkhos from the mouth of the Indus to the head of the Persian Gulf. Arrian's narrative, copied from the Journal of the voyage written by Nearkhos himself, forms an admirable supplement to the Periplûs, as it contains a minute description of a part of the Erythræan Coast which is merely glanced at by the author of that work. The translations have been prepared from the most approved texts. The notes, in a few instances only, bear upon points of textual criticism, their main object being to present in a concise form for popular reading the most recent results of learned enquiry directed to verify, correct, or otherwise illustrate the contents of the narratives.

The warm and unanimous approbation bestowed upon the first volume of this series, both by the Press in this country and at home, has given me great encouragement to proceed with the undertaking, and a third volume is now in preparation, to contain the *Indika* of Ktêsias and the account of India given by Strabo in the 15th Book of his Geography.

Patna College, June 1879.

PERIPLUS OF THE ERYTHRÆAN SEA.

INTRODUCTION.[1]

The *Periplûs of the Erythræan Sea* is the title prefixed to a work which contains the best account of the commerce carried on from the Red Sea and the coast of Africa to the East Indies during the time that Egypt was a province of the Roman empire. The Erythræan Sea was an appellation given in those days to the whole expanse of ocean reaching from the coast of Africa to the utmost boundary of ancient knowledge on the East—an appellation in all appearance deduced from the entrance into it by the Straits of the Red Sea, styled Erythra by the Greeks, and not excluding the Gulf of Persia.

The author was a Greek merchant, who in the first century of the Christian era had, it would appear, settled at Berenîkê, a great seaport situated in the southern extremity of Egypt, whence he made commercial voyages which carried him to the seaports of Eastern Africa as far as Azania, and to those of Arabia as far as Kanê, whence, by taking advantage of the south-west monsoon, he crossed over to the ports lying on the western shores of India. Having made careful

---

[1] The Introduction and Commentary embody the main substance of Müller's Prolegomena and Notes to the *Periplûs*, and of Vincent's *Commerce and Navigation of the Ancients* so far as it relates specially to that work. The most recent authorities accessible have, however, been also consulted, and the result of their inquiries noted. I may mention particularly Bishop Caldwell's Dravidian Grammar, to which I am indebted for the identification of places on the Malabar and Coromandel coasts.

a

observations and inquiries regarding the navigation and commerce of these countries, he committed to writing, for the benefit of other merchants,
the knowledge which he had thus acquired. Much
cannot be said in praise of the style in which he
writes. It is marked by a rude simplicity, which
shows that he was not a man of literary culture,
but in fact a mere man of business, who in com-
posing restricts himself to a narrow round of set
phrases, and is indifferent alike to grace, freedom,
or variety of expression. It shows further that
he was a Greek settled in Egypt, and that he must
have belonged to an isolated community of his
countrymen, whose speech had become corrupt by
much intercourse with foreigners. It presents a
very striking contrast to the rhetorical diction
which A g a t h a r k h i d ê s, a great master of all
the tricks of speech, employs in his description of
the Erythræan. For all shortcomings, however,
in the style of the work, there is ample compensa-
tion in the fulness, variety, accuracy, and utility
of the information which it conveys. Such indeed
is its superiority on these points that it must be
reckoned as a most precious treasure: for to it
we are indebted far more than to any other work
for most of our knowledge of the remote shores of
Eastern Africa, and the marts of India, and the
condition of ancient commerce in these parts of
the world.

The name of the author is unknown. In the Heidelberg MS., which alone has preserved the little
work, and contains it after the *Periplûs* of Arrian,
the title given is Ἀρριανοῦ περίπλους τῆς Ἐρυθρᾶς
θαλάσσης. Trusting to the correctness of this

title, Stuckius attributed the work to A r r i a n of
Nikomedia, and Fabricius to another Arrian who
belonged to Alexandria. No one, however, who
knows how ancient books are usually treated can
fail to see what the real fact here is, viz. that
since not only the *Periplûs Maris Erythræi*, but
also the *Anonymi Periplûs Ponti Euxini* (whereof
the latter part occurs in the Heidelberg MS. before
Arrian's *Ponti Periplûs*) are attributed to Arrian,
and the different Arrians are not distinguished
by any indications afforded by the titles, there can
be no doubt that the well-known name of the
Nikomedian writer was transferred to the books
placed in juxtaposition to his proper works, by
the arbitrary judgment of the librarians. In fact
it very often happens that short works written by
different authors are all referred to one and the
same author, especially if they treat of the same
subject and are published conjointly in the same
volume. But in the case of the work before us,
any one would have all the more readily ascribed
it to Arrian who had heard by report anything
of the *Paraplûs* of the Erythræan Sea described
in that author's *Indika*. On this point there
is the utmost unanimity of opinion among
writers.

That the author, whatever may have been his
name, lived in Egypt, is manifest. Thus he says
in § 29: "Several of the trees *with us* in Egypt
weep gum," and he joins the names of the
Egyptian months with the Roman, as may be
seen by referring to §§ 6, 39, 49, and 56. The place
in which he was settled was probably Berenikê,
since it was from that port he embarked on his

voyages to Africa and Arabia, and since he speaks
of the one coast as on the right from Berenîkê,
and the other on the left. The whole tenor of the
work proclaims that he must have been a merchant.
That the entire work is not a mere compilation
from the narratives or journals of other merchants
and navigators, but that the author had himself
visited some of the seats of trade which he describes, is in itself probable, and is indicated in § 20,
where, contrary to the custom of the ancient
writers, he speaks in his own person :—" In sailing
south, therefore, *we* stand off from the shore and
keep *our* course down the middle of the gulf."
Compare with this what is said in § 48 : τὰ πρὸς
τὴν ἐμπορίαν τὴν ἡμετέραν.

As regards the age to which the writer belonged : it is first of all evident that he wrote after the
times of Augustus, since in § 23 mention is made
of the Roman Emperors. That he was older,
however, than P t o l e m y the Geographer, is
proved by his geography, which knows nothing of
India beyond the Ganges except the traditional
account current from the days of Eratosthenês to
those of Pliny, while it is evident that Ptolemy
possessed much more accurate information regarding these parts. It confirms this view that
while our author calls the island of Ceylon P a l a i-
s i m o u n d o u, Ptolemy calls it by the name
subsequently given to it—S a l i k ê. Again, from
§ 19, it is evident that he wrote before the
kingdom of the Nabathæans was abolished by
the Romans. Moreover Pliny (VI. xxvi. 104), in
proceeding to describe the navigation to the
marts of India by the direct route across the

ocean with the wind called Hippalos, writes to
this effect :—" And for a long time this was the
mode of navigation, until a merchant discovered
a compendious route whereby India was brought
so near that to trade thither became very lucrative. For, every year a fleet is despatched, carrying on board companies of archers, since the
Indian seas are much infested by pirates. Nor
will a description of the whole voyage from Egypt
tire the reader, since now for the first time correct
information regarding it has been made public."
Compare with this the statement of the *Periplûs*
in § 57, and it will be apparent that while this
route to India had only just come into use in the
time of Pliny, it had been for some time in use in
the days of our author. Now, as Pliny died in
79 A.D., and had completed his work two years
previously, it may be inferred that he had written
the 6th book of his *Natural History* before our
author wrote his work. A still more definite in-
dication of his date is furnished in § 5, where
Zoskalês is mentioned as reigning in his
times over the Auxumitæ. Now in a list of the
early kings of Abyssinia the name of Za-
Hakale occurs, who must have reigned from
77 to 89 A.D. This Za-Hakale is doubtless
the Zoskalês of the *Periplûs*, and was the
contemporary of the emperors Vespasian, Titus,
and Domitian. We conclude, therefore, that the
Periplûs was written a little after the death of
Pliny, between the years A.D. 80-89.

Opinions on this point, however, have varied
considerably. Salmasius thought that Pliny and
our author wrote at the same time, though their ac-

counts of the same things are often contradictory.
In support of this view he adduces the statement
of the *Periplûs* (§ 54), "M u z i r i s, a place in India,
is in the kingdom of Kêprobotres," when compared with the statement of Pliny (VI. xxvi. 104),
" C œ l o b o t h r a s was reigning there when I
committed this to writing;" and argues that since
K ê p r o b o t r a s and C œ l o b o t h r a s are but
different forms of the same name, the two authors
must have been contemporary. The inference is,
however, unwarrantable, since the name in question, like that of P a n d î ô n, was a common appellation of the kings who ruled over that part of India.

Dodwell, again, was of opinion that the *Periplûs*
was written after the year A. D. 161, when Marcus
Aurelius and Lucius Verus were joint emperors.
He bases, in the first place, his defence of this view
on the statement in § 26 : "Not long before our
own times the Emperor (Καῖσαρ) destroyed the
place," viz. E u d a i m ô n-A r a b i a, now Aden.
This emperor he supposes must have been Trajan,
who, according to Eutropius (VIII. 3), reduced
Arabia to the form of a province. Eutropius, however, meant by Arabia only that small part of it
which adjoins Syria. This Dodwell not only denies,
but also asserts that the conquest of Trajan embraced the whole of the Peninsula—a sweeping
inference, which he bases on a single passage
in the *Periplûs* (§ 16) where the south part
of Arabia is called ἡ πρώτη Ἀραβία, " the First
Arabia." From this expression he gathers that
Trajan, after his conquest of the country, had
divided it into several provinces, designated according to the order in which they were consti-

tuted. The language of the *Periplûs*, however, forbids us to suppose that there is here any reference to a Roman province. What the passage states is that A z a n i a (in Africa) was by ancient right subject to the kingdom τῆς πρώτης γινομένης (λεγομένης according to Dodwell) 'Αραβίας, and was ruled by the despot of M a p h a r i t i s.

Dodwell next defends the date he has fixed on by the passage in § 23, where it is said that K h a-r i b a ë l sought by frequent gifts and embassies to gain the friendship of the emperors (τῶν αὐτοκρατόρων). He thinks that the time is here indicated when M. Aurelius and L. Verus were reigning conjointly, A.D. 161-181. There is no need, however, to put this construction on the words, which may without any impropriety be taken to mean '*the emperors for the time being,*' viz. Vespasian, Titus, and Domitian.

Vincent adopted the opinion of Salmasius regarding the date of the work, but thinks that the Kaïsar mentioned in § 26 was Claudius. "The Romans," he says, "from the time they first entered Arabia under Ælius Gallus, had always maintained a footing on the coast of the Red Sea. They had a garrison at L e u k ê K ô m ê, in Nabathæa, where they collected the customs; and it is apparent that they extended their power down the gulf and to the ports of the ocean in the reign of Claudius, as the freedman of A n n i u s P l o c a m u s was in the act of collecting the tributes there when he was carried out to sea and over to T a p r o b a n ê. If we add to this the discovery of Hippalus in the same reign, we find a better reason for the destruction of Aden at this time than at any other." The assertion in this extract that the garrison and custom-house at L e u k ê K ô m ê belonged to the Romans is not warranted by the language of the *Periplûs*, which in fact shows that they belonged to M a l i k h o s the king of the Nabathæans. Again, it is a mere conjecture that the voyage which the freedman of Plocamus (who, according to Pliny, farmed the revenues of the Red Sea) was making along the coast of Arabia, when he was carried away by the monsoon to Taprobanê, was a voyage undertaken to collect the revenues due to the Roman treasury. With regard to the word Καῖσαρ, which has occasioned so much perplexity, it is most probably a corrupt reading in a text notorious for its corruptness. The proper reading may perhaps be ΕΛΙΣΑΡ. At any rate, had one of the emperors in reality destroyed Aden, it is unlikely that their historians would have failed to mention such an important fact.

Schwanbeck, although he saw the weakness of the arguments with which Salmasius and Vincent endeavoured to establish their position, nevertheless thought that our author lived in the age of Pliny and wrote a little before him, because those particulars regarding the Indian navigation which Pliny says became known in his age agree, on the whole, so well with the statement in the *Periplûs* that they must have been extracted therefrom. No doubt there are, he allows, some discrepancies; but those, he thinks, may be ascribed to the haste or negligence of the copyist. A careful examination, however, of parallel passages in Pliny and the *Periplûs* show this assertion to be untenable. Vincent himself speaks with caution on this point :—" There is," he says, " no absolute proof that either copied from the other. But those who are acquainted with Pliny's methods of abbreviation would much rather conclude, if one must be a copyist, that his title to this office is the clearest."

From these preliminary points we pass on to consider the contents of the work, and these may be conveniently reviewed under the three heads Geography, Navigation, Commerce. In the commentary, which is to accompany the translation, the Geography will be examined in detail. Meanwhile we shall enumerate the voyages which are distinguishable in the *Periplús*,[a] and the articles of commerce which it specifies.

I. VOYAGES MENTIONED IN THE PERIPLUS.

I. A voyage from *Bereníké*, in the south of Egypt, down the western coast of the Red Sea through the Straits, along the coast of Africa, round Cape Guardafui, and then southward along the eastern coast of Africa as far as Rhâpta, a place about six degrees south of the equator.

II. We are informed of two distinct courses confined to the Red Sea : one from Myos Hormos, in the south of Egypt, across the northern end of the sea to Leukê Kômê, on the opposite coast of Arabia, near the mouth of the Elanitic Gulf, whence it was continued to Mouza, an Arabian port lying not far westward from the Straits ; the other from Bereníké directly down the gulf to this same port

---

[a] The enumeration is Vincent's, altered and abridged.

b

III. There is described next to this a voyage from the mouth of the Straits along the southern coast of Arabia round the promontory now called Ras-el-Had, whence it was continued along the eastern coast of Arabia as far as Apologos (now Oboleh), an important emporium at the head of the Persian Gulf, near the mouth of the river Euphrates.

IV. Then follows a passage from the Straits to India by three different routes: the first by adhering to the coasts of Arabia, Karmania, Gedrosia, and Indo-Skythia, which terminated at B a r u g a z a (Bharôch), a great emporium on the river N a m m a d i o s (the Narmadâ), at a distance of thirty miles from its mouth; the second from Kanê, a port to the west of S u a g r o s, a great projection on the south coast of Arabia, now Cape Fartaque; and the third from Cape Guardafui, on the African side—both across the ocean by the monsoon to M o u z i r i s and N e l k u n d a, great commercial cities on the coast of Malabar.

V. After this we must allow a similar voyage performed by the Indians to Arabia, or by the Arabians to India, previous to the performance of it by the Greeks, because the Greeks as late as the reign of Philomêtôr met this commerce in Sabæa.

VI. We obtain an incidental knowledge of a voyage conducted from ports on the east coast of Africa over to India by the monsoon long before Hippalos introduced the knowledge of that wind to the Roman world. This voyage was connected, no doubt, with the commerce of Arabia, since the Arabians were the great traffickers of antiquity, and held in subjection part of the sea-board of Eastern

Africa. The Indian commodities imported into
Africa were rice, ghee, oil of sesamum, sugar,
cotton, muslins, and sashes. These commodities,
the *Periplûs* informs us, were brought sometimes
in vessels destined expressly for the coast of Africa,
while at others they were only part of the cargo,
out of vessels which were proceeding to another
port. Thus we have two methods of conducting
this commerce perfectly direct; and another
by touching on this coast with a final destination to Arabia. This is the reason that the
Greeks found cinnamon and the produce of India
on this coast, when they first ventured to pass
the Straits in order to seek a cheaper market than
Sabæa.

II. Articles of Commerce mentioned in the Periplus.

I. Animals :—

1. Παρθένοι εὐειδεῖς πρὸς παλλακίαν—Handsome
girls for the haram, imported into Barugaza for
the king (49).[3]

2. Δούλικα κρείσσονα—Tall slaves, procured at
Opônê, imported into Egypt (14).

3. Σώματα θηλυκὰ—Female slaves, procured
from Arabia and India, imported into the island
of Dioskoridês (31).

4. Σώματα.—Slaves imported from Omana and
Apologos into Barugaza (36), and from Moundou
and Malaô (8, 9).

5. Ἵπποι—Horses imported into Kanê for the
king, and into Mouza for the despot (23, 24).

---

[3] The numerals indicate the sections of the *Periplûs* in
which the articles are mentioned.

6. ' Ἡμίοναι νωτηγοί—Sumpter mules imported into Mouza for the despot (24).

II. Animal Products :—

1. Βούτυρον—Butter, or the Indian preparation therefrom called ghî, a product of Ariakê (41); exported from Barugaza to the Barbarine markets beyond the Straits (14). The word, according to Pliny (xxviii. 9), is of Skythian origin, though apparently connected with Βοῦς, τυρός. The reading is, however, suspected by Lassen, who would substitute Βόσμορον or Βόσπορον, a kind of grain.χ

2. Δέρματα Σηρικὰ—Chinese hides or furs. Exported from Barbarikon, a mart on the Indus (39). Vincent suspected the reading δέρματα, but groundlessly, for Pliny mentions the Sêres sending their iron along with vestments and hides (vestibus pellibusque), and among the presents sent to Yudhishṭhira by the Śaka, Tushâra and Kaṅka skins are enumerated.—Mahâbh. ii. 50, quoted by Lassen.

3. Ἐλέφας—Ivory. Exported from Adouli (6), Aualitês (8), Ptolemaïs (3), Mossulon (10), and the ports of Azania (16, 17). Also from Barugaza (49), Mouziris and Nelkunda (56); a species of ivory called Βωσαρὴ is produced in Desarênê (62).

4. Ἔριον Σηρικὸν—Chinese cotton. Imported from the country of the Thînai through Baktria to Barugaza, and by the Ganges to Bengal, and thence to Dimurikê (64). By Ἔριον Vincent seems to understand silk in the raw state.

5. Κέρατα—Horns. Exported from Barugaza to the marts of Omana and Apologos (36). Müller suspects this reading, thinking it strange that

13

such an article as *horns* should be mentioned
between *wooden beams* and *logs*. He thinks, therefore, that Κέρατα is either used in some technical
sense, or that the reading Κορμῶν or Κορμίων
should be substituted—adding that Κορμοὺς ἐβένου,
planks of ebony, are at all events mentioned by
Athênaios (p. 201a) where he is quoting Kal-
lixenos of Rhodes.

6. Κοράλλιον—Coral. (Sans. *pravâla*, Hindi
mûngâ.) Imported into Kanê (28), Barbarikon
on the Indus (39), Barugaza (49), and Naoura,
Tundis, Mouziris, and Nelkunda (56).

7. Λάκκος χρωμάτινος—Coloured lac. Exported
to Adouli from Ariakê (6). The Sanskrit word
is *lâkshâ*, which is probably a later form of *râkshâ*,
connected, as Lassen thinks, with *râga*, from the
root *ranj*, to dye. The vulgar form is *lâkkha*.
Gum-lac is a substance produced on the leaves
and branches of certain trees by an insect, both
as a covering for its egg and food for its young.
It yields a fine red dye.[a] Salmasius thinks that
by λάκκος χρωμάτινος must be understood not lac
itself, but vestments dyed therewith.

8. Μαργαρίτης—Pearl. (Sans. *mukta*, Hindi,
moti.) Exported in considerable quantity and of
superior quality from Mouziris and Nelkunda (56).
Cf. πινικόν.

9. Νῆμα Σηρικόν—Silk thread. From the coun-

---

[a] Bhagvânlâl Indrâji Pandit points out that the colour is
called *alaktaka*, Prakrit *alito*: it is used by women for
dying the nails and feet,—also as a dye. The *gulall* or
pill-like balls used by women are made with arrowroot
coloured with *alito*, and cotton dipped in it is sold in the
bazars under the name of *pothi*, and used for the same
purposes. He has also contributed many of the Sanskrit
names, and some notes.

try of the Thinai: imported into Barugaza and the marts of Dimurikê (64). Exported from Barugaza (49), and also from Barbarikon on the Indus (39)." It is called μέταξα by Procopius and all the later writers, as well as by the *Digest*, and was known without either name to Pliny."—Vincent.

10. Πινίκιος κόγχος—the Pearl-oyster. (Sans. *śukti*.) Fished for at the entrance to the Persian Gulf (35). Pearl (πίνικον) inferior to the Indian sort exported in great quantity from the marts of Apologos and Omana (36). A pearl fishery (Πινικοῦ κολύμβησις) in the neighbourhood of Kolkhoi, in the kingdom of Pandiôn, near the island of Epiodôros; the produce transported to Argalou, in the interior of the country, where muslin robes with pearl inwoven (μαργαρίτιδες σινδόνες) were fabricated (59). The reading of the MS. is σινδόνες, ἐβαργαρείτιδες λεγόμεναι, for which Salmasius proposed to read μαργαρίτιδες. Müller suggests instead αἱ Ἀργαρίτιδες, as if the muslin bore the name of the place *Argarou* or *Argulou*, where it was made.

Pearl. is also obtained in Taprobanê (61); is imported into the emporium on the Ganges called Gangê (63).

11. Πορφύρα—Purple. Of a common as well as of a superior quality, imported from Egypt into Mouza (24) and Kanê (28), and from the marts of Apologos and Omana into Barugaza (36).

12. Ῥινόκερως—Rhinoceros (Sans. *khadgaḍ*)—the horn or the teeth, and probably the skin. Exported from Adouli (16), and the marts of Azania (7). Bruce found the hunting of the rhinoceros still a trade in Abyssinia.

13. Χελώνη—Tortoise (Sans. *kachchhapa*) or tortoise-shell. Exported from Adouli (6) and Aualitês (7); a small quantity of the genuine and land tortoise, and a white sort with a small shell, exported from Ptolemaïs (3); small shells (Χελανάρια) exported from Mossulon (10); a superior sort in great quantity from Opônê (13); the mountain tortoise from the island of Menouthias (15); a kind next in quality to the Indian from the marts of Azania (16, 17); the genuine, land, white, and mountain sort with shells of extraordinary size from the island of Dioskoridês (30, 31); a good quantity from the island of Serapis (33); the best kind in all the Erythræan—that of the Golden Khersonêsos (63), sent to Mouziris and Nelkunda, whence it is exported along with that of the islands off the coast of Dimurikê (probably the Laccadive islands) (56); tortoise is also procured in Taprobanê (61).

III.—Plants and their products:—

1. Ἀλόη—the aloe (Sans. *agaru*). Exported from Kanê (28). The sort referred to is probably the bitter cathartic, not the aromatic sort supposed by some to be the sandalwood. It grows abundantly in Sokotra, and it was no doubt exported thence to Kanê. "It is remarkable," says Vincent, "that when the author of the *Periplûs* arrives at Sokotra he says nothing of the aloe, and mentions only Indian cinnabar as a gum or resin distilling from a tree: but the confounding of cinnabar with dragon's-blood was a mistake of ancient date and a great absurdity" (II. p. 689).

2. Ἀρώματα—aromatics (εὐωδία, θυμιάματα.) Exported from Aualitês (7), Mossulon (10). Among

the spices of Tabai (12) are enumerated ἀσύβη καί ἄρωμα καί μάγλα, and similarly among the commodities of Opônê κασσία καὶ ἄρωμα καὶ μότω ; and in these passages perhaps a particular kind of aromatic (cinnamon ?) may by preëminence be called ἄρωμα. The occurrence, however, in two instances of such a familiar word as ἄρωμα between two outlandish words is suspicious, and this has led Müller to conjecture that the proper reading may be ἀρηβὼ, which Salmasius, citing Galen, notes to be a kind of cassia.

3. Ασύβη—Asuphê, a kind of cassia. Exported from Tabai (12). "This term," says Vincent, "if not Oriental, is from the Greek ἀσύφηλος, signifiying *cheap* or *ordinary* ; but we do not find ἀσύφη used in this manner by other authors : it may be an Alexandrian corruption of the language, or it may be the abbreviation of a merchant in his invoice." (*Asafœtida*, Sans. *hingu* or *bâhlika*, Mar, *hing*.)

4. Βδέλλα, (common form Βδέλλιον). Bdella, Bdellium, produced on the sea-coast of Gedrosia (37); exported from Barbarikon on the Indus (39); brought from the interior of India to Barugaza (48) for foreign export (49). Bdella is the gum of the *Balsamodendron Mukul*, a tree growing in Sind, Kâthiâvâḍ, and the Dîsâ district.[b] It is used both as an incense and as a cordial medicine. The bdellium of Scripture is a crystal, and has nothing in common with the bdellium of the *Periplûs* but its transparency. Conf. Dioskorid. i. 80 ; Plin. xii. 9; Galen, *Therapeut. ad Glauc*. II. p. 106 ; Lassen,

---

[b] Sans. *Guggula*, Guj. *Gûgal*, used as a tonic and for skin and urinary diseases.—B. I. P.

Ind. Alt. vol. I. p. 290; Vincent, vol. II. p. 690; Yule's *Marco Polo*, vol. II. p. 387. The etymology of the word is uncertain. Lassen suspects it to be Indian.

5. Γίζειρ—Gizeir, a kind of cassia exported from Tabai (12). This sort is noticed and described by Dioskoridês.

6. Δόκος—Beams of wood. Exported from Barugaza to the marts of Omana and Apologos (36). (? Blackwood.)

7. Δούακα—Douaka, a kind of cassia. Exported from Malaó and Moundou (8, 9). It was probably that inferior species which in Dioskorid. i. 12, is called δάκαρ or δακάρ or δάρκα.

8. Ἐβένιναι φάλαγγες—Logs of ebony (*Diospyros melanoxylon.*) Exported from Barugaza to the marts of Omana and Apologos (36).

9. Ἔλαιον—Oil (*tila*). Exported from Egypt to Adouli (6); ἔλαιον σησάμινον, oil of sêsamê, a product of Ariakê (41). Exported from Barugaza to the Barbarine markets (14), and to Moskha in Arabia (32).[a]

10. Ἰνδικὸν μέλαν—Indigo. (Sans. *nîlî*, Guj. *gulî*.) Exported from Skythic Barbarikon (39). It appears pretty certain that the culture of the indigo plant and the preparation of the drug have been practised in India from a very remote epoch. It has been questioned, indeed, whether the Indicum mentioned by Pliny (xxxv. 6) was indigo, but, as it would seem, without any good reason. He states that it was brought from India, and that when diluted it produced an admirable mixture

---

[a] Mahuwâ oil (Guj. *doliuñ*, Sans. *madhuka*) is much exported from Bharoch.—B. I. P.

c

of blue and purple colours. *Vide* McCulloch's *Commer. Dict.* s. v. *Indigo.* Cf. Salmas. in *Exerc.* Plin. p. 181. The dye was introduced into Rome only a little before Pliny's time.

11. Κάγκαμον—Kankamon. Exported from Malao and Moundou (8, 10). According to Dioskoridês i. 23, it is the exudation of a wood, like myrrh, and used for fumigation. Cf. Plin. xii. 44. According to Scaliger it was gum-lac used as a dye. It is the "dekamalli" gum of the bazars.

12. Κάρπασος—Karpasus (Sans. *kárpása'*; Heb. *karpas*,) *Gossypium arboreum*, fine muslin—a product of Ariakê (41). "How this word found its way into Italy, and became the Latin *carbasus*, fine linen, is surprising, when it is not found in the Greek language. The Καρπάσιον λίνον of Pausanias (*in Atticis*), of which the wick was formed for the lamp of Pallas, is asbestos, so called from Karpasos, a city of Crete—Salmas. Plin. *Exercit.* p. 178. Conf. Q. Curtius viii. 9 :—' Carbaso Indi corpora usque ad pedes velant, eorumque rex lecticâ margaritis circumpendentibus recumbit distinctis auro et purpurâ carbasis quâ indutus est.' " Vincent II. 699.

13. Κασσία or Κασία (Sans. *kuta*, Heb. *kiddah* and *keziah*). Exported from Tabai (12); a coarse kind exported from Malao and Moundou (8, 9); a vast quantity exported from Mossulon and Opônê (10, 13).

"This spice," says Vincent, "is mentioned frequently in the *Periplûs*, and with various additions, intended to specify the different sorts properties, or appearances of the commodity. It is a species of cinnamon, and manifestly the same as what we call cinnamon at this day; but dif-

ferent from that of the Greeks and Romans,
which was not a bark, nor rolled up into pipes,
like ours. Theirs was the tender shoot of the
same plant, and of much higher value." "If our
cinnamon," he adds, "is the ancient casia, our casia
again is an inferior sort of cinnamon." Pliny
(xii. 19) states that the cassia is of a larger size
than the cinnamon, and has a thin rind rather
than a bark, and that its value consists in being
hollowed out. Dioskoridês mentions cassia as a
product of Arabia, but this is a mistake, Arabian
cassia having been an import from India. Herodotos (iii.) had made the same mistake, saying
that cassia grew in Arabia, but that cinnamon
was brought thither by birds from the country
where Bacchus was born (India). The cassia
shrub is a sort of laurel. There are ten kinds of
cassia specified in the *Periplûs*.[1] Cf. Lassen, *Ind.
Alt.* I. 279, 283 ; Salmas. *Plin. Exercit.* p. 1304 ;
Galen, *de Antidotis*, bk. i.

14. Κιννάβαρι Ἰνδικὸν—Dragon's-blood, *damu'l
akhaweia* of the Arabs, a gum distilled from
Pterocarpus Draco, a leguminous tree[2] in the
island of Dioskoridês or Sokotra (30). Cinnabar, with which this was confounded, is the red
sulphuret of mercury. Pliny (lib. xxix. c. 8)
distinguishes it as 'Indian cinnabar.' Dragon's-
blood is one of the concrete balsams, the produce
of *Calamus Draco*, a species of rattan palm of
the Eastern Archipelago, [of *Pterocarpus Draco*,
allied to the Indian Kino tree or *Pt. marsupium* of

[1] May not some of these be the fragrant root of the *kusâ
grass, Andropogon calamus—aromaticus* ?—J. B.
[2] A similar gum is obtained from the *Pálâsa* (Guj. *khâ-
kharu*), the *Dhâka* of Râjputâna.—B. I. P.

South India, and of *Dracæna Draco*, a liliaceous
tree of Madeira and the Canary Islands].

15. Κόστος (Sansk. *kushṭa*, Mar. *choka*, Guj.
kaṭha and *pushkara mûla*,)—Kostus. Exported
from Barbarikon, a mart on the Indus (39), and
from Barugaza, which procured it from Kâbul
through Proklaïs, &c. This was considered the
best of aromatic roots, as nard or spikenard was
· the best of aromatic plants. Pliny (xii. 25) describes this root as hot to the taste and of con-
summate fragrance, noting that it was found at
the head of Patalênê, where the Indus bifurcates
to form the Delta, and that it was of two sorts)
black and white, black being of an inferior quality. Lassen states that two kinds are found in
India—one in Multân, and the other in Kâbul and
Kâśmîr. " The Costus of the ancients is still
exported from Western India, as well as from
Calcutta to China, under the name of *Putchok*, to
be burnt as an incense in Chinese temples. Its
identity has been ascertained in our own days by
Drs. Royle and Falconer as the root of a plant
which they called *Aucklandia Costus*. . . . . . .·
Alexander Hamilton, at the beginning of last century, calls it *ligna dulcis* (sic), and speaks of it as an
export from Sind, as did the author of the *Periplûs*
1600 years earlier." Yule's *Marco Polo*, vol. II.
p. 388.

16. Κρόκος—Crocus, Saffron. (Sans. *kaśmîraja*,
Guj. *kesir*, Pers. *zafrân*.) Exported from Egypt to
Mouza (24) and to Kanê (28).

17. Κύπερος—Cyprus. Exported from Egypt to
Mouza (24). It is an aromatic rush used in medicine (Pliny xxi. 18). Herodotos (iv. 71) describes

it as an aromatic plant used by the Skythians for embalming. Κύπερος is probably Ionic for Κύπειρος—Κύπειρος Ἰνδικὸς of Dioskoridês, and *Cypria herba indica* of Pliny.—Perhaps Turmeric, *Curcuma longa,* or Galingal possibly.

18. Λέντια, (Lat. *lintea*)—Linen. Exported from Egypt to Adouli (6).

19. Λίβανος (Heb. *lebonah,* Arab. *luban,* Sans. *śrīvāsa*)—Frankincense. Peratic or Libyan frankincense exported from the Barbarine markets—Tabai (12), Mossulon (10), Malaô and Moundou, in small quantities (8, 9); produced in great abundance and of the best quality at Akannai (11); Arabian frankincense exported from Kanê (28). A magazine for frankincense on the Sakhalitic Gulf near Cape Suagros (30). Moskha, the port whence it was shipped for Kanê and India (32) and Indo-Skythia (39).

Regarding this important product Yule thus writes :—"The coast of Hadhramaut is the true and ancient Χώρα λιβανοφόρος or λιβανωτοφόρος, indicated or described under those names by Theophrastus, Ptolemy, Pliny, Pseudo-Arrian, and other classical writers, *i.e.* the country producing the fragrant gum-resin called by the Hebrews *Lebonah,* by the Arabs *Luban* and *Kundur,* by the Greeks *Líbanos,* by the Romans *Thus,* in mediæval Latin *Olibanum* (probably the Arabic *al-luban,* but popularly interpreted as *oleum Libani*), and in English frankincense, *i.e.* I apprehend, 'genuine incense' or 'incense proper.'* It is still produced in this

---

* What the Bráhmans call *kundaru* is the gum of a tree called the *Dhúpa-salai*; another sort of it, from Arabia, they call *Istsa,* and in Káthiáwád it is known as *Sesagundar.*—B. I. P.

region and exported from it, but the larger part of
that which enters the markets of the world is
exported from the roadsteads of the opposite
Sumâlî coast. Frankincense when it first exudes
is milky white; whence the name *white incense* by
which Polo speaks of it, and the Arabic name
lubau apparently refers to milk. The elder Niebuhr,
who travelled in Arabia, depreciated the Libanos
of Arabia, representing it as greatly inferior to that
brought from India, called Benzoin. He adds that
the plant which produces it is not native, but
originally from Abyssinia."—*Marco Polo*, vol. II.
p. 443, &c.

20. Λύκιον—Lycium. Exported from Barbarikon in Indo-Skythia (39), and from Barugaza (49).
Lycium is a thorny plant, so called from being
found in Lykia principally. Its juice was used for
dying yellow, and a liquor drawn from it was
used as a medicine (Celsus v. 26, 30, and vi. 7).
It was held in great esteem by the ancients. Pliny
(xxiv. 77) says that a superior kind of Lycium
produced in India was made from a thorn called
also *Pyxacanthus* (box-thorn) *Chironia*. It is known
in India as *Ruzót*, an extract of the *Berberis
lycium* and *B. aristata*, both grown on the Himâlayas. Conf. the λύκιον ἰνδικὸν of Dioskor. i. 133.
(? Gamboge.)

21. Μάγλα—Magla—a kind of cassia mentioned
only in the *Periplûs*. Exported from Tabai (12).

22. Μάκειρ—Macer. Exported from Malaô and
Moundou (8, 9). According to Pliny, Dioskoridês,
and others, it is an Indian bark—perhaps a kind of
cassia. The bark is red and the root large. The
bark was used as a medicine in dysenteries. Pliny

xii. 8; Salmasius, 1302. (? The *Karachâlâ* of the bâzârs, *Kutajatvak*).

23. Μαλάβαθρον (Sans. *tamâlapattra*, the leaf of the *Laurus Cassia*), Malabathrum, Betel. Obtained by the Thinai from the Sesatai and exported to India[10] (65); conveyed down the Ganges to Gangê near its mouth (63); conveyed from the interior of India to Mouziris and Nelkunda for export (56). That Malabathrum was not only a masticatory, but also an unguent or perfume, may be inferred from Horace (*Odes*, II. vii. 89):—

. . . " coronatus nitentes
    Malabathro Syrio capillos",

and from Pliny (xii. 59): " Dat et Malabathrum Syria, arborum folio convoluto, arido colore, ex quo exprimitur oleum ad unguenta: fertiliore ejusdem Egypto: laudatius tamen ex India venit." From Ptolemy (VII. ii. 16) we learn that the best Malabathrum was produced in Kirrhadia—that is, Rangpur. Dioskoridês speaks of it as a masticatory, and was aware of the confusion caused by mistaking the nard for the betel.

24. Μέλι τὸ καλάμινον, τὸ λεγόμενον σάκχαρ (Sans. *śarkará*, Prâkrit *śákara*, Arab. *sukkar*, Latin *saccharum*)—Honey from canes, called Sugar. Exported from Barugaza to the marts of Barbaria (14). The first Western writer who mentions this article was Theophrastos, who continued the labours of Aristotle in natural history. He called it a sort of honey extracted from reeds. Strabo states, on the authority of Nearkhos, that reeds in India yield honey without bees.

[10] More likely from Nepâl, where it is called *tejapât*.— B. I. P.

Ælian (*Hist. Anim.*) speaks of a kind of honey pressed from reeds which grew among the Prasii. Seneca (Epist. 84) speaks of sugar as a kind of honey found in India on the leaves of reeds, which had either been dropped on them from the sky as dew, or had exuded from the reeds themselves. This was a prevalent error in ancient times, *e.g.* Dioskoridês says that sugar is a sort of concreted honey found upon canes in India and Arabia Felix, and Pliny that it is collected from canes like a gum. He describes it as white and brittle between the teeth, of the size of a hazel-nut at most, and used in medicine only. So also Lucan, alluding to the Indians near the Ganges, says that they quaff sweet juices from tender reeds. Sugar, however, as is well known, must be extracted by art from the plant. It has been conjectured that the sugar described by Pliny and Dioskoridês was sugar candy obtained from China.

25. Μελίλωτον—Melilot, Honey-lotus. Exported from Egypt to Barugaza (49). Melilot is the Egyptian or Nymphæa Lotus, or Lily of the Nile, the stalk of which contained a sweet nutritive substance which was made into bread. So Vincent ; but Melilot is a kind of clover, so called from the quantity of honey it contains. The nymphæa lotus, or what was called the Lily of the Nile, is not a true lotus, and contains no edible substance.

26. Μοκρότον. Exported from Moundou (9) and Mossulon (10). It is a sort of incense, mentioned only in the *Periplûs*.

27. Μότω—Motô—a sort of cassia exported from Tabai and Opônê (13).

28. Μύρον—Myrrh. (Sans. *bola.*) Exported from

Egypt to Barugaza as a present for the king (49).
It is a gum or resin issuing from a thorn found
in Arabia Felix, Abyssinia, &c., *vide σμύρνη inf.*

29. Νάρδος (Sans. *nalada,* ' kaskas,' Heb. *nerd*)
Nard, Spikenard.[11] Gangetic spikenard brought
down the Ganges to Gangê, near its mouth (63), and
forwarded thence to Mouziris and Nelkunda (56).
Spikenard produced in the regions of the Upper
Indus and in Indo-Skythia forwarded through
Ozênê to Barugaza (48). Imported by the Egyp-
tians from Barugaza and Barbarikon in Indo-
Skythia (49, 39).

The *Nardos* is a plant called (from its root
being shaped like an ear of corn) νάρδου στάχυς,
also ναρδόσταχυς, Latin *Spica nardi,* whence ' spikenard.' It belongs to the species *Valeriana.* " No
Oriental aromatic," says Vincent, " has caused
greater disputes among the critics or writers on
natural history, and it is only within these few
years that we have arrived at the true knowledge
of this curious odour by means of the inquiries
of Sir W. Jones and Dr. Roxburgh. Pliny describes the nard with its *spica,* mentioning also
that both the leaves and the *spica* are of high
value, and that the odour is the prime in all
unguents; the price 100 denarii for a pound. But
he afterwards visibly confounds it with the Malabathrum or Betel, as will appear from his usage
of *Hadrosphœrum, Mesosphœrum,* and *Microsphœ-
rum,* terms peculiar to the Betel"—II. 743-4. See
Sir W. Jones on the spikenard of the ancients in
As. Res. vol. II. pp. 416 *et seq.,* and Roxburgh's

---

[11] Obtained from the root of *Nardostachys jatamansi,* a
native of the eastern Himâlayas.—J. B.

d

additional remarks on the spikenard of the ancients, vol. IV. pp. 97 *et seq.*, and botanical observations on the spikenard, pp. 433. See also Lassen,
Ind. Alt. vol. I. pp. 288 *et seq.*

30. Ναύπλιος—Nauplius. Exported in small
quantity from the marts of Azania (17). The
signification of the word is obscure, and the reading suspected. For NaΥΠλιος Müller suggests
NaΡΓΙλιος, the Indian cocoanut, which the Arabians
call *Nargil* (Sansk. *nárikéla* or *nálikéra*, Guj.
náliyér, Hindi *náliyar*). It favours this sugges-
tion that cocoanut oil is a product of Zangibar, and
that in four different passages of Kosmas Indiko-
pleustês nuts are called ἀργέλλια, which is either a
corrupt reading for ναργέλλια, or Kosmas may not
have known the name accurately enough.

31. 'Οθόνιον—Muslin. Sêric muslin sent from
the Thînai to Barugaza and Dimurikê (64). Coarse
cottons produced in great quantity in Ariakê,
carried down from Ozênê to Barugaza (48) ; large
supplies sent thither from Tagara also (51) ;
Indian muslins exported from the markets of
Dimurikê to Egypt (56). Muslins of every description, Seric and dyed of a mallow colour, exported from Barugaza to Egypt (49); Indian muslin
taken to the island of Dioskoridês (31); wide Indian
muslins called μοναχή, *monákhé*, i. e. of the best
and finest sort; and another sort called σαγματογήνη, *sagmatogênê*, i. e. coarse cotton unfit for
spinning, and used for stuffing beds, cushions, &c.,
exported from Barugaza to the Barbarine markets
(14), and to Arabia, whence it was exported to
Adouli (6). The meanings given to *monákhé* and
sagmatogênê (for which other readings have

been suggested) are conjectural. Vincent defends
the meaning assigned to *sagmatogêné* by a quotation from a passage in Strabo citing Nearkhos:—" Fine muslins are made of cotton, but the
Makedonians use cotton for flocks, and stuffing
of couches."

32. 'Οῖνοs—Wine. Laodikean and Italian wine
exported in small quantity to Adouli (6); to Aualitês (7), Malaô (8), Mouza (24), Kanê (28), Barbarikon in Indo-Skythia (39); the same sorts,
together with Arabian wine, to Barugaza (49);
sent in small quantity to Mouziris and Nelkunda
(56); the region inland from Oraia bears the vine
(37), which is found also in the district of Mouza
(24), whence wine is exported to the marts of
Azania, not for sale, but to gain the good will of
the natives (17). Wine is exported also from
the marts of Apologos and Omana to Barugaza
(36). By Arabian wine may perhaps be meant
palm or toddy wine, a great article of commerce.

33. Ὄμφακοs Διοσπολιτικῆs χυλόs—the juice of
the sour grape of Diospolis. Exported from
Egypt to Aualitês (7). This, says Vincent, was
the *dipse* of the Orientals, and still used as a
relish all over the East. *Dipse* is the rob of
grapes in their unripe state, and a pleasant acid.—
II. 751. This juice is called by Dioskoridês (iv. 7)
in one word Ομφάκιον, and also (v. 12) 'Οῖνοs
'Ομφακίτηs. Cf. Plin. xii. 27.

34 Ὄρυζα (Sansk. *vríhi*)—Rice. Produced in
Oraia and Ariakê (37, 41), exported from Barugaza to the Barbarine markets (14), and to the
island of Dioskoridês (31).

35. Πέπερι (Sansk. *pippalí,*) long pepper—Pep-

per. Kottonarik pepper exported in large quantities from Mouziris and Nelkunda (56); long pepper from Barugaza (49). *Kottonara* was the name of the district, and *Kottonarikon* the name of the pepper for which the district was famous. Dr. Buchanan identifies Kottonara with Kadattanâḍu, a district in the Calicut country celebrated for its pepper. Dr. Burnell, however, identifies it with Kolatta-Nâḍu, the district about Tellicherry, which, he says, is the pepper district.

36. Πυρὸs—Wheat. Exported in small quantity from Egypt to Kanê (28), some grown in the district around Mouza (24).

37. Σάκχαρι—Sugar : see under Μέλι.

38. Σανδαράκη—Sandarakê (*chandrasa* of the bazars) ; a resin from the *Thuja articulata* or *Callitris quadrivalvis*, a small coniferous tree of North Africa; it is of a faint aromatic smell and is used as incense. Exported from Egypt to Barugaza (49); conveyed to Mouziris and Nelkunda (56).[13]

Sandarakê also is a red pigment—red sulphuret of arsenic, as orpiment is the yellow sulphuret. Cf. Plin. xxxv. 22, Hard. "Juba informs us that sandarace and ochre are found in an island of the Red Sea, Topazas, whence they are brought to us."

39. Σαντάλινα and σασάμινα ξύλα—Logs of Sandal and Sasame (*santalum album*). Exported from Barugaza to the marts of Omana and Apologos (36). Σαντάλινα is a correction of the MS. reading σαγάλινα proposed by Salmasius. Kosmas Indiko-

[13] It is brought now from the Eastern Archipelago.— B. I. P.

pleustes calls sandalwood τζαδάνα. For σασάμινα
of the MS. Stuckius proposed σησάμινα—a futile
emendation, since sesame is known only as a
leguminous plant from which an oil is expressed,
and not as a tree. But possibly Red Saunders
wood (*Pterocarpus Santalinus*) may be meant.

40. Σησάμινον ἔλαιον. See Ἔλαιον.

41. Σινδόνες διαφορώταται αἱ Γαγγητικᾶι. The finest
Bengal muslins exported from the Ganges (63);
other muslins in Taprobanê (61); Μαργαρίτιδες (?),
made at Argalou and thence exported (59);
muslins of all sorts and mallow-tinted (μολόχιναι)
sent from Ozênê to Barugaza (48), exported thence
to Arabia for the supply of the market at Adouli
(6).

42. Σῖτος—Corn. Exported from Egypt to
Adouli (7), Malaô (8); a little to Mouza (24), and to
Kanê (28), and to Muziris and Nelkunda for ships'
stores (56); exported from Dimurikê and Ariakê
into the Barbarine markets (14), into Moskha (32)
and the island of Dioskoridês (31); exported also
from Mouza to the ports of Azania for presents (17).

43. Σμύρνη—Myrrh (vide μύρον). Exported from
Malaô, Moundou, Mossulon (8, 9, 10); from Aualitês
a small quantity of the best quality (7); a choice
sort that trickles in drops, called *Abeirminaia*
(ἐκλεκτὴ καὶ στακτὴ ἀβειρμιναία), exported from Mouza
(24). For Ἀβειρμιναία of the MS. Müller suggests
to read γαβειρμιναία, inclining to think that two
kinds of myrrh are indicated, the names of which
have been erroneously combined into one, viz. the
Gabiræan and Minæan, which are mentioned by
Dioskoridês, Hippokratês, and Galen. There is a
Wadi Gabir in Omân.

44. Στύραξ—Storax (Sans. *turuska*, *selarasa* of the bazars),—one of the balsams. Exported from Egypt to Kanê (28), Barbarikon on the Indus (39), Barugaza (40). Storax is the produce of the tree *Liquidambar orientale*, which grows in the south of Europe and the Levant.[13] The purest kind is storax in grains. Another kind is called *styrax calamita*, from being brought in masses wrapped up in the leaves of a certain reed. Another kind, that sold in shops, is semi-fluid.

45. Φοῖνιξ—the Palm or Dates. Exported from the marts of Apologos and Omana to Barugaza (36, 37).

IV.—Metals and Metallic Articles :—

1. Ἀργυρᾶ σκεύη, ἀργυρώματα—Vessels of silver. Exported from Egypt to Mossulon (10), to Barbarikon on the Indus (39). Silver plate chased or polished (τορνευτὰ or τετορνευμένα) sent as presents to the despot of Mouza (24), to Kanê for the king (28). Costly (βαρύτιμα) plate to Barugaza for the king (49). Plate made according to the Egyptian fashion to Adouli for the king (6).

2. Ἀρσενικὸν—Arsenic (*somal*). Exported from Egypt to Mouziris and Nelkunda (56).

3. Δηνάριον—Denary. Exported in small quantity from Egypt to Adouli (6). Gold and silver denarii sent in small quantity to the marts of Barbaria (8, 13); exchanges with advantage for native money at Barugaza (49).

The *denary* was a Roman coin equal to about 8½*d.*, and a little inferior in value to the Greek drachma.

4. Κάλτις—Kaltis. A gold coin (νομισμὰ) cur-

---

[13] In early times it was obtained chiefly from *Styrax officinalis*, a native of the same region.—J. B.

rent in the district of the Lower Ganges (63);
Benfey thinks the word is connected with the
Sanskṛit *kalita,* i.e. *numeratum.*

5. Κασσίτερος (Sans. *baṅga, kathila*)—Tin.
Exported from Egypt to Aualitês (7), Malaô (8)
Kanê (28), Barugaza (49), Mouziris and Nelkunda
(56). India produced this metal, but not in those
parts to which the Egyptian trade carried it.

6. Μόλυβδος—Lead (Sansk. *nága,* Guj. *sísuṅ*).
Exported from Egypt to Barugaza, Muziris, and
Nelkunda (49, 56).

7. 'Ορείχαλκος—Orichalcum (Sans. *tripus,* Prak.
pítala)—Brass. Used for ornaments and cut into
small pieces by way of coin. Exported from Egypt
to Adouli (6).

The word means 'mountain copper.' Ramusio
calls it white copper from which the gold and
silver have not been well separated in extracting
it from the ore. Gold, it may be remarked, does
not occur as an export from any of the African
marts, throughout the *Periplús.*

8. Σίδηρος, σιδηρᾶ σκεύη—Iron, iron utensils.
Exported from Egypt to Malaô, Moundou, Tabai,
Opônê (8, 9, 12, 13). Iron spears, swords and
adzes exported to Adouli (6). Indian iron and
sword-blades (στόμωμη) exported to Adouli from
Arabia (Ariakê?). Spears (λόγχαι) manufactured
at Mouza, hatchets (πελύκια), swords (μάχαιραι),
awls (ὀπέτια) exported from Mouza to Azania
(17).

On the Indian sword see Ktêsias, p. 80, 4.
The Arabian poets celebrate swords made of Indian
steel. Cf. Plin. xxxiv. 41 :—" Ex omnibus autem
generibus palma Serico ferro est." This iron, as

has already been stated, was sent to India along with skins and cloth. Cf. also Edrisi, vol. I. p. 65, ed. Joubert. Indian iron is mentioned in the Pandects as an article of commerce.

9. Στίμμι—Stibium (Sans. *sauwírânjana*, Prâk. *surmâ*). Exported from Egypt to Barugaza (49), to Mouziris and Nelkunda (56).

Stibium is a sulphuret of antimony, a dark pigment, called *kohol*, much used in the East for dyeing the eyelids.

10. Χαλκὸς—Copper (Sans. *tâmra*) or Brass. Exported from Egypt to Kanê (28), to Barugaza (49), Mouziris and Nelkunda (56). Vessels made thereof (Χαλκουργήματα) sent to Mouza as presents to the despot (24). Drinking-vessels (ποτήρια) exported to the marts of Barbaria (8, 13). Big and round drinking-cups to Adouli (6). A few (μελίεφθα ὀλίγα) to Malaô (8) ; μελίεφθα χαλκᾶ for cooking with, and being cut into bracelets and anklets for women to Adouli (6).

Regarding μελίεφθα Vincent says : "No usage of the word occurs elsewhere ; but metals were prepared with several materials to give them colour, or to make them tractable, or malleable. Thus χολόβαφα in Hesychius was brass prepared with ox's gall to give it the colour of gold, and used, like our tinsel ornaments or foil, for stage dresses and decorations. Thus common brass was neither ductile nor malleable, but the Cyprian brass was both. And thus perhaps brass, μελίεφθα was formed with some preparation of honey." Müller cannot accept this view. "It is evident," he says, "that the reference is to ductile copper from which, as Pliny says, all impurity has been carefully removed by smelting, so that pots, bracelets, and articles of that sort could be fabricated from it. One might therefore think that the reading should be περίεφθα or πυρίεφθα, but in such a case the writer would have said περίεφθον χαλκόν. In vulgar speech μελίεφθα is used as a substantive noun, and I am therefore almost persuaded that, just as molten copper, ὁ χαλκὸς ὁ χυτὸς, *cuprum caldarium*, was called τρόχιος, from the likeness in shape of its round masses to hoops, so *laminæ* of ductile copper (*plaques de cuivre*) might have been called μελίεφθα, because shaped like thin honey-cakes, πέμματα μελίεφθα."

11. Χρυσὸς—Gold. Exported from the marts of Apologos and Omana to Barugaza (36). Gold plate—χρυσώματα—exported from Egypt to Mouza for the despot (24), and to Adouli for the king (6).

V. Stones :—

1. Λιθία διαφανὴς — Gems (carbuncles ?) found in Taprobanê (63) ; exported in every variety from Mouziris and Nelkunda (56).

2. Ἀδάμας—Diamonds. (Sans. *vajra*, *píraka*). Exported from Mouziris and Nelkunda (56).

3. Καλλεανὸς λίθος—Gold-stone, yellow crystal, chrysolith ? Exported from Barbarikon in Indo-Skythia (39).

It is not a settled point what stone is meant. Lassen says that the Sanskrit word *kalydṇa* means *gold*, and would therefore identify it with the chrysolith or gold-stone. If this view be correct, the reading of the MS. need not be altered into καλλαϊνὸς, as Salmasius, whom the editors of the *Periplûs* generally follow, enjoins. In support of the alteration Salmasius adduces Pliny, xxxvii.

e

56 :—" Callais sapphirum imitatur, candidior et litoroso mari similis. Callainas vocant e turbido Callaino", and other passages. Schwanbeck, however, maintaining the correctness of the MS. reading, says that the Sanskṛit word *kalyâṇa* generally signifies *money*, but in a more general sense *anything beautiful*, and might therefore have been applied to this gem. *Kalyâṇa*, he adds, would appear in Greek as καλλιαιὸς or καλλεανὸς rather than καλλαϊνὸς. In like manner *kalyâṇi* of the Indians appears in our author not as καλλάϊνα, but, as it ought to be, καλλίενα.

4. Λύγδος—Alabaster. Exported from Mouza (24). Salmasius says that an imitation of this alabaster was formed of Parian marble, but that the best and original *lygdus* was brought from Arabia, that is, Mouza, as noted in the *Periplûs*. Cf. Pliny (xxxvi. 8) :— " Lygdinos in Tauro repertos . . . antea ex Arabia tantum advehi solitos candoris eximii."

5. Ὀνυχινὴ λίθια—Onyx (*akika*—agate). Sent in vast quantities (πλείστη) from Ozênê and Paithana to Barugaza (48, 51), and thence exported to Egypt (49). Regarding the onyx mines of Gujarât *vide* Ritter, vol. VI. p. 603.

6. Μουρρίνη, sup. λιθία—Fluor-spath. Sent from Ozênê to Barugaza, and exported to Egypt (49). Porcelain made at Diospolis (μουρρίνη λιθία ἡ γενομένη ἐν Διοσπόλει) exported from Egypt to Adouli (6).

The reading of the MS. is μοῤῥίνης. By this is to be understood *vitrum murrhinum*, a sort of china or porcelain made in imitation of cups or vases of *murrha*, a precious fossil-stone resembling, if not identical with, *fluor-spath*, such as is found in Derbyshire. Vessels of this stone were exported from India, and also, as we learn from Pliny, from Karmania, to the Roman market, where they fetched extravagant prices.[14] The " cups baked in Parthian fires" (*pocula Parthis focis cocta*) mentioned by Propertius (IV. v. 26) must be referred to the former class. The whole subject is one which has much exercised the pens of the learned. " Six hundred writers," says Müller, " emulously applying themselves to explain what had the best claim to be considered the *murrha* of the ancients, have advanced the most conflicting opinions. Now it is pretty well settled that the murrhine vases were made of that stone which is called in German *flusspath* (*spato-fluore*)". He then refers to the following as the principal authorities on the subject :—Pliny—xxxiii. 7 *et seq.*; xxxiii. *proœm.* Suetonius—*Oct.* c. 71; Seneca—*Epist.* 123; Martial—iv. 86; xiv. 43; · *Digest*—xxxiii. 10, 3; xxxiv. 2. 19; Rozière—*Mémoire sur les Vases murrhins*, &c.; in *Description de l'Égypt*, vol. VI. pp. 277 *et seq.*; Corsi—*Delle Pietre antiche*, p. 106; Thiersch—*Ueber die Vasa Murrhina der Alten*, *in Abhandl. d. Munchn. Akad.* 1835, vol. I. pp. 443-509; A learned Englishman in the *Classical Journal* for 1810, p. 472; Witzsch in Pauly's *Real Encycl.* vol. V. p. 253; See also Vincent, vol. II. pp. 723-7.

7. 'Οψιανὸς λίθος—the Opsian or Obsidian stone, found in the Bay of Hanfelah (5). Pliny says,— "The opsians or obsidians are also reckoned as a

---

[14] Nero gave for one 300 talents = £58,125. They were first seen at Rome in the triumphal procession of Pompey. [May these not have been of emerald, or even ruby ?—J. B.]

sort of glass bearing the likeness of the stone which Obsius (or Obsidius) found in Ethiopia, of a very black colour, sometimes even translucent, hazier than ordinary glass to look through, and when used for mirrors on the walls reflecting but shadows instead of distinct images." (Bk. xxxvi. 37). The only Obsius mentioned in history is a M. Obsius who had been Prætor, a friend of Germanicus, referred to by Tacitus (*Ann.* IV. 68, 71). He had perhaps been for a time prefect of Egypt, and had coasted the shore of Ethiopia at the time when Germanicus traversed Egypt till he came to the confines of Ethiopia. Perhaps, however, the name of the substance is of Greek origin—'οψιανός, from its reflecting power.

8. Σάπφειρος—the Sapphire. Exported from Barbarikon in Indo-Skythia (39). "The ancients distinguished two sorts of dark blue or purple, one of which was spotted with gold. Pliny says it is never pellucid, which seems to make it a different stone from what is now called sapphire."— Vincent (vol. II. p. 757), who adds in a note, " Dr. Burgess has specimens of both sorts, the one with gold spots like lapis lazuli, and not transparent."[15]

9. 'Υάκινθος—Hyacinth or Jacinth. Exported from Mouziris and Nelkunda (56). According to Salmasius this is the Ruby. In Solinus xxx. it would seem to be the Amethyst (Sánsk. *pushkardja.*)

10. 'Υαλος 'αργή—Glass of a coarse kind. Exported from Egypt to Barugaza (49), to Mouziris and Nelkunda (56). Vessels of glass (ὑαλὰ σκεύη) ex-

---

[15] Possibly the Lapis Lazuli is meant.—J. B.

ported from Egypt to Barbarikon in Indo-Skythia
(39). Crystal of many sorts (λιθίας ὑαλῆς πλεῖστα
γένη) exported from Egypt to Adouli, Aualitês,
Mossulon (6, 7, 10) ; from Mouza to Azania (17).

11. Χρυσόλιθος—Chrysolite. Exported from
Egypt to Barbarikon in Indo-Skythia (39), to
Barugaza (43), to Mouziris and Nelkunda (56).
Some take this to be the topaz (Hind. *píroją́*).

VI. Wearing Apparel :—

1. 'Ιμάτια ἄγναφα—Cloths undressed. Manufactured in Egypt and thence exported to Adouli (6).
These were disposed of to the tribes of Barbaria
—the Troglodyte shepherds of Upper Egypt,
Nubia and Ethiopia.

2. 'Ιμάτια βαρβαρικὰ σύμμικτα γεγναμμένα—
Cloths for the Barbarine markets, dressed and
dyed of various colours. Exported to Malaô and
Aualitês (8, 7).

3. 'Ιματισμὸς 'Αραβικὸς—Cloth or coating for the
Arabian markets. Exported from Egypt (24).
Different kinds are enumerated :—Χειριδωτὸς, with
sleeves reaching to the wrist ; 'Ότε ἁπλοῦς καὶ ὁ
κοινὸς, with single texture and of the common sort ;
σκοτουλάτος, wrought with figures, checkered ; the
word is a transliteration of the Latin *scutulatus*,
from *scutum*, the checks being lozenge-shaped, like
a shield : see Juvenal, Sat. ii. 79 ; διάχρυσος, shot
with gold ; πολυτελὴς, a kind of great price sent
to the despot of Mouza ; Κοινὸς καὶ ἁπλοῦς καὶ
ὁ νόθος, cloth of a common sort, and cloth of simple
texture, and cloth in imitation of a better commodity, sent to Kanê (28) ; Διάφορος ἁπλοῦς, of
superior quality and single texture, for the king
(28) ; 'Απλοῦς, *of single texture*, in great quantity, and

νόθος, an inferior sort imitating a better, in small quantity, sent to Barbarikon in Indo-Skythia (39), 'απλοῦς καὶ νόθος παντοῖος, and for the king ἁπλοῦς πολυτελής, sent to Barugaza (49); 'Ιματισμὸς οὐ πολύς—cloth in small quantity sent to Muziris and Nelkunda (56); ἐντόπιος, of native manufacture, exported from the marts of Apologos and Omana to Barugaza (36).

4. 'Αβόλλαι—Riding or watch cloaks. Exported from Egypt to Mouza (34), to Kanê (28). This word is a transliteration of the Latin *Abolla*. It is supposed, however, to be derived from Greek: ἀμβολλη, i. e. ἀμφιβολή. · It was a woollen cloak of close texture—often mentioned in the Roman writers: *e.g.* Juven. *Sat.* iii. 115 and iv. 76; Sueton. *Calig.* c. 35. Where the word occurs in sec. 6 the reading of the MS. is ἄβολοι, which Müller has corrected to ἀβόλλαι, though Salmasius had defended the original reading.

5. Δικρόσσια (Lat. *Mantilia utrinque fimbriata*) —Cloths with a double fringe. Exported from Egypt to Adouli (6). This word occurs only in the *Periplûs*. The simple Κρόσσιον, however, is met with in Herodian, *Epim.* p. 72. An adjective δίκροσσος is found in Pollux vii. 72. "We cannot err much," says Vincent, "in rendering the δικρόσσια of the *Periplûs* either *cloth fringed*, with Salmasius, or *striped*, with Apollonius. Meursius says λεντία ἄκροσσα are *plain linens not striped.*

6. Ζώναι πολύμιτοι πηχυαῖοι—Flowered or embroidered girdles, a cubit broad. Exported from Egypt to Barugaza (49). Σκιωταὶ—girdles (*kácha*) shaded of different colours, exported to Mouza (24). This word occurs only in the *Periplûs*.

7. Καυνάκαι—Garments of frieze. Exported from Arabia to Ádouli (6); a pure sort—ἁπλοῖ—exported to the same mart from Egypt (6). In the latter of these two passages the MS. reading is γαυνάκαι. Both forms are in use: conf. Latin *gaunace*—Varro, *de L. L.* 4, 35. It means also *a fur garment* or *blanket—vestis stragula*.

8. Λώδικες—Quilts or coverlids. Exported in small quantity from Egypt to Mouza (24) and Kanê (28).

9. Περιζώματα—Sashes, girdles, or aprons. Exported from Barugaza to Adouli (6), and into Barbaria (14).

10. Πολύμιτα—Stuffs in which several threads were taken for the woof in order to weave flowers or other objects: Latin *polymita* and *plumatica*. Exported from Egypt to Barbarikon in Indo-Skythia (39), to Mouziris and Nelkunda (56).

11. Σάγοι 'Αρσινοητικοὶ γεγναμμένοι καὶ βεβαμμένοι—Coarse cloaks made at Arsinoê, dressed and dyed. Exported from Egypt to Barbaria (8, 13).

12. Στολαὶ 'Αρσινοητικαὶ—Women's robes made at Arsinoê. Exported from Egypt to Adouli (6).

13. Χιτῶνες—Tunics. Exported from Egypt to Malaô, Moundou, Mossulon (8, 9, 10).

VII. In addition to the above, works of art are mentioned.

'Ανδριάντες—Images, sent as presents to Kharibaël (48). Cf. Strabo (p. 714), who among the articles sent to Arabia enumerates τόρευμα, γραφὴν, πλάσμα, pieces of sculpture, painting, statues.

Μουσικά—Instruments of music, for presents to the king of Ariakê (49).

ANONYMI [ARRIANI UT FERTUR] PERIPLUS MARIS ERYTHRÆI.

1. The first of the important roadsteads established on the Red Sea, and the first also of the great trading marts upon its coast, is the port of M y o s-h o r m o s in Egypt. Beyond it

---

Commentary.

(1) M y o s H o r m o s.—Its situation is determined by the cluster of islands now called Jifâtîn [lat. 27° 12′ N., long. 33° 55′ E.] of which the three largest lie opposite an indenture of the coast of Egypt on the curve of which its harbour was situated [near Ras Abu Somer, a little north of Safâjah Island]. It was founded by Ptolemy Philadelphos B. c. 274, who selected it as the principal port of the Egyptian trade with India in preference to Arsinoe,[16] N. N. E. of Suez, on account of the difficulty and tediousness of the navigation down the Heroöpolite Gulf. The vessels bound for Africa and the south of Arabia left its harbour about the time of the autumnal equinox, when the North West wind which then prevailed carried them quickly down the Gulf. Those bound for the Malabar Coast or Ceylon left in July, and if they cleared the Red Sea before the 1st of

---

[16] There was another Arsinoe between Ras Dh'ib and Ras Shukhair, lat. 28° 3′ N. The few geographical indications added by Mr. Burgess to these comments as they passed through the press are enclosed in brackets. [ ]

at a distance of 1800 stadia is B e r e n î k ê, which is to your right if you approach it by sea.

September, they had the monsoon to assist their passage across the ocean. M y o s H o r m o s was distant from K o p t o s [lat. 26° N.], the station on the Nile through which it communicated with Alexandria, a journey of seven or eight days along a road opened through the desert by Philadelphos. The name M y o s H o r m o s is of Greek origin, and may signify either the Harbour of the Mouse, or, more probably, of the Mussel, since the pearl mussel abounded in its neighbourhood. A g a t h a r k h i d ê s calls it A p h r o d i t ē s H o r m o s, and Pliny V e n e r i s P o r t u s. [Veneris Portus however was probably at Sherm Sheikh, lat. 24° 36′ N. Off the coast is Wade Jemâl Island, lat. 24° 39′ N., long. 35° 8′ E., called Iambe by Pliny, and perhaps the Aphroditês Island of Ptolemy IV. v. 77.] Referring to this name Vincent says: "Here if the reader will advert to Aphroditê, the Greek title of Venus, as springing from the foam of the ocean, it will immediately appear that the Greeks were translating here, for the native term to this day is *Saffauge-el-Bahri*, 'sponge of the sea'; and the vulgar error of the sponge being the foam of the sea, will immediately account for Aphroditê."

The rival of Myos-Hormos was B e r e n i k ê, a city built by Ptolemy Philadelphos, who so named it in honour of his mother, who was the daughter of Ptolemy Lagos and Antigonê. It was in the same parallel with Syênê and therefore not far from the Tropic [lat. 23° 55′ N.]. It stood nearly

j

These roadsteads are both situate at the furthest
end of Egypt, and are bays of the Red Sea.

2. The country which adjoins them on the
right below Berenîkê is B a r b a r i a. Here the
sea-board is peopled by the I k h t h y o p h a g o i,
who live in scattered huts built in the narrow
gorges of the hills, and further inland are the

---

at the bottom of *Foul Bay* (ἐν βάθει τοῦ 'Ακαθάρτου
Κόλπου), so called from the coast being foul with
shoals and breakers, and not from the impurity of
its water, as its Latin name, *Sinus Immundus,* would
lead us to suppose. Its ruins are still per-
ceptible even to the arrangement of the streets,
and in the centre is a small Egyptian temple
adorned with hieroglyphics and bas-reliefs of
Greek workmanship. Opposite to the town is
a very fine natural harbour, the entrance of which
has been deep enough for small vessels, though
the bar is now impassable at low water. Its prosperity under the Ptolemies and afterwards under
the Romans was owing to its safe anchorage and
its being, like Myos-Hormos, the terminus of a
great road from Koptos along which the traffic
of Alexandria with Ethiopia, Arabia, and India
passed to and fro. Its distance from K o p t o s
was 258 Roman miles or 11 days' journey. The
distance between Myos-Hormos and Berenikê is
given in the *Periplûs* at 225 miles, but this is
considerably above the mark. The difficulty of
the navigation may probably have made the
distance seem greater than it was in reality.

(2) Adjoining B e r e n i k ê was B a r b a r i a

Berbers, and beyond them the Agriopha-
goi and Moskhophagoi, tribes under
regular government by kings Beyond these
again, and still further inland towards the west
[is situated the metropolis called Meroê].

3. Below the Moskhophagoi, near the
sea, lies a little trading town distant from Bere-

(ἡ Βαρβαρικὴ χώρα)—the land about Ras Abû
Fatima [lat. 22° 26′ N.—Ptol. IV. vii. 28]. The
reading of the MS. is ἡ Τισηβαρικὴ which Müller
rejects because the name nowhere occurs in any
work, and because if Barbaria is not mentioned here, our author could not afterwards
(Section 5) say ἡ ἄλλη Βαρβαρία. The Agrio-
phagoi who lived in the interior are mentioned
by Pliny (vi. 35), who says that they lived principally on the flesh of panthers and lions. Vincent
writes as if instead of Αγριοφάγων the reading
should be Ακριδοφάγων locust-eaters, who are
mentioned by Agatharkhidês in his *De Mari
Erythraeo*, Section 58. Another inland tribe
is mentioned in connection with them—the Moskhophagoi, who may be identified with the
Rizophagoi or Spermatophagoi of
the same writer, who were so named because they
lived on roots or the tender suckers and buds
of trees, called in Greek μόσχοι. This being a
term applied also to the young of animals,
Vincent was led to think that this tribe fed on
the brinde or flesh cut out of the living animal as
described by Bruce.

(3) To the south of the Moskhophagoi lies
Ptolemaïs Thêrôn, or, as it is called by

nîkĕ about 4000 stadia, called Ptolemaïs
Thêrôn, from which, in the days of the
Ptolemies, the hunters employed by them used
to go up into the interior to catch elephants. In
this mart is procured the true (or marine)
tortoise-shell, and the land kind also, which,
however, is scarce, of a white colour, and smaller
size. A little ivory is also sometimes obtainable, resembling that of Adouli. This place
has no port, and is approachable only by boats.

Pliny, Ptolemaïs Epitheras. [On Er-rih
island, lat. 18° 9′ N., long 38° 27′ E., are the ruins
of an ancient town—probably Ptolemaïs Therôn,—
Müller however places Suche here.—Ptol. I.
viii. 1.; IV. vii. 7 ; VIII. xvi. 10]. It was originally an Ethiopian village, but was extended
and fortified by Ptolemy Philadelphos, who made
it the depôt of the elephant trade, for which its
situation on the skirts of the great Nubian forest,
where these animals abounded, rendered it pecu-
liarly suitable. The Egyptians before this had
imported their elephants from Asia, but as the
supply was precarious, and the cost of importa-
tion very great, Philadelphos made the most
tempting offers to the Ethiopian elephant-hunters
(Elephantophagoi) to induce them to abstain from
eating the animal, or to reserve at least a portion
of them for the royal stables. They rejected
however all his solicitations, declaring that even
for all Egypt they would not forego the luxury of
their repast. The king resolved thereupon to procure his supplies by employing hunters of his own.

4. Leaving Ptolemaïs Thêrôn we are conducted, at the distance of about 3000 stadia, to A d o u l i, a regular and established port of trade situated on a deep bay the direction of which is

---

(4) Beyond P t o l e m a ï s T h ê r ô n occur A d o u l ê, at a distance, according to the *Periplûs*, of 3000 stadia—a somewhat excessive estimate. The place is called also A d o u l e i and more commonly Adoulis by ancient writers (Ptol. IV. vii. 8; VIII. xvi. 11). It is represented by the modern Thulla or Zula [pronounced Azule,—lat. 15° 12′—15° 15′ N., long. 39° 36′ E.].—To the West of this, according to Lord Valentia and Mr. Salt, there are to be found the remains of an ancient city. It was situated on the A d o u l i k o s K o l p o s (Ptol. I. xv. 11.; IV. vii. 8), now called Annesley Bay, the best entrance into Abyssinia. It was erroneously placed by D'Anville at Dokhnau or Harkiko, close to Musawwâ [lat. 15° 35′ N.] There is much probability in the supposition that it was founded by a party of those Egyptians who, as we learn from Herodotos (II. 30), to the number of 240,000 fled from their country in the days of Psammêtikhos (B. C. 671—617) and went to as great a distance beyond Meroë, the capital of Ethiopia, as Meroë is beyond Elephantinê. This is the account which Pliny (VI. 3-4) gives of its foundation, adding that it was the greatest emporium of the T r o g l o d y t e s, and distant from P t o l e m a ï s a five days' voyage, which by the ordinary reckoning is 2,500 stadia. It was an emporium for rhinoceros' hides, ivory and tortoise-shell. It had not only a large sea-borne traffic, but was also a

due south. Facing this, at a distance seaward
of about 200 stadia from the inmost recess of
the bay, lies an island called O r e i n ê (or ' the
mountainous'), which runs on either side parallel

---

caravan station for the traffic of the interior of
Africa. Under the Romans it was the haven
of A u x u m ê (Ptol. IV. vii. 25,—written also
Auxumis, Axumis), now Axum, the capital of the
kingdom of Tigre in Abyssinia. A u x u m ê was
the chief centre of the trade with the interior of
Africa in gold-dust, ivory, leather, hides and
aromatics. It was rising to great prosperity
and power about the time the *Periplûs* was
written, which is the earliest work extant in which
it is mentioned. It was probably founded by the
Egyptian exiles already referred to. Its remaining monuments are perfectly Egyptian and not
pastoral, Troglodytik, Greek, or Arabian in their
character. Its name at the same time retains
traces of the term A s m a k, by which, as we
learn from Herodotos, those exiles were designated, and Heeren considers it to have been one
of the numerous priest-colonies which were sent
out from Meroë.

At Adouli was a celebrated monument, a
throne of white marble with a slab of basanite
stone behind it, both covered with Greek characters, which in the sixth century of our era were
copied by K o s m a s I n d i k o p l e u s t ê s. The
passage in Kosmos relating to this begins
thus: "A d u l ê is a city of Ethiopia and the
port of communication with A x i ô m i s, and the
whole nation of which that city is the capital.

with the mainland. Ships, that come to trade with Adouli, now-a-days anchor here, to avoid being attacked from the shore; for in former times when they used to anchor at the very head of the bay, beside an island called D i o d ô r o s, which was so close to land that the sea was fordable, the neighbouring barbarians, taking advantage of this, would run across to attack the ships at their moorings. At the distance of 20 stadia from the sea, opposite O r e i n ê, is the village of Adouli, which is not of any great size, and inland from this a three

---

In this port we carry on our trade from Alexandria and the Elanitik Gulf. The town itself is about a mile from the shore, and as you enter it on the Western side which leads from A x i ô m i s, there is still remaining a chair or throne which appertained to one of the Ptolemys who had subjected this country to his authority." The first portion of the inscription records that Ptolemy Euergetês (247-222 B.C.) received from the Troglodyte Arabs and Ethiopians certain elephants which his father, the second king of the Makedonian dynasty, and himself had taken in hunting in the region of A d u l ê and trained to war in their own kingdom. The second portion of the inscription commemorates the conquests of an anonymous Ethiopian king in Arabia and Ethiopia as far as the frontier of Egypt. A d o u l i, it is known for certain, received its name from a tribe so designated which formed a part of the D a n a- k i l shepherds who are still found in the neigh-

days' journey is a city, K o l ö ê, the first
market where ivory can be procured. From
Kolöê it takes a journey of five days to reach the
metropolis of the people called the A u x u m i-
t a i, whereto is brought, through the province
called K y ê n e i o n, all the ivory obtained on
the other side of the Nile, before it is sent on to
Adouli. The whole mass, I may say, of the elephants and rhinoceroses which are killed *to supply
the trade* frequent the uplands *of the interior*,
though at rare times they are seen near the coast,
even in the neighbourhood of Adouli. Besides
the islands already mentioned, a cluster consist-

---

bourhood of Annesley Bay, in the island of Diset
[lat. 15° 28′, long. 39° 45′, the Diodôros perhaps
of the *Periplûs*] opposite which is the town or
station of Masawâ (anc. Saba) [lat. 15° 37′ N.,
long. 39° 28′ E.], and also in the archipelago of
D h a l a k, called in the *Periplûs*, the islands of
A l a l a i o u. The merchants of Egypt, we learn
from the work, first traded at Masawwâ but afterwards removed to Oreine for security. This is an
islet in the south of the Bay of Masawwâ, lying
20 miles from the coast; it is a rock as its name
imports, and is of considerable elevation.

A d u l i being the best entrance into Abyssinia,
came prominently into notice during the late
Abyssinian war. Beke thus speaks of it, " In our
recent visit to Abyssinia I saw quite enough to
confirm the opinion I have so long entertained,
that when the ancient Greeks founded Adule or
Adulis at the mouth of the river Hadâs, now only

ing of many small ones lies out in the sea to the
right of this port. They bear the name of
A l a l a i o u , and yield the tortoises with which
the I k h t h y o p h a g o i supply the market.

5. Below Adouli, about 800 stadia, occurs
another very deep bay, at the entrance of which
on the right are vast accumulations of sand, wherein is found deeply embedded the Opsian stone,
which is not obtainable anywhere else. The
king of all this country, from the M o s k h o-
p h a g o i to the other end of B a r b a r i a , is
Z ô s k a l ê s , a man at once of penurious

---

a river bed except during the rains, though a
short way above there is rain all the year round,
they knew that they possessed one of the keys of
Abyssinia.''

(5) At a distance of about 100 miles beyond
A d o u l i the coast is indented by another bay now
known as H a n f e l a h bay [near Râs Hanfelah in
lat. 14° 44′, long. 40° 49′ E.] about 100 miles from
Annesley Bay and opposite an island called Daramsas
or Hanfelah. It has wells of good water and a small
lake of fresh water after the rains ; the coast is inhabited by the Dummoeta, a tribe of the Danakil].
This is the locality where, and where only, the Opsian
or Obsidian stone was to be found. Pliny calls it an
unknown bay, because traders making for the ports
of Arabia passed it by without deviating from
their course to enter it. He was aware, as well as
our author, that it contained the Opsian stone, of
which he gives an account, already produced in the
introduction.

g

habits and of a grasping disposition, but otherwise honourable in his dealings and instructed in the Greek language.

6. The articles which these places import are the following :—

'Ιμάτια βαρβαρικὰ, ἄγναφα τὰ ἐν 'Αιγύπτῳ γινόμενα —Cloth undressed, of Egyptian manufacture, for the Barbarian market.

Στολὰι 'Αρσινοητικὰι—Robes manufactured at Arsinoē.

'Αβόλλαι νόθοι χρωμάτιναι—Cloaks, made of a poor cloth imitating a better quality, and dyed.

Λέντια—Linens.

Δικρόσσια—Striped cloths and fringed. Mantles with a double fringe.

Λιθίας ὑαλῆς πλείονα γένη καὶ ἄλλης μορρίνης, τῆς γινομένης ἐν Διοσπόλει—Many sorts of glass or crystal, and of that other transparent stone called Myrrhina, made at Diospolis.

'Ορείχαλκος—Yellow copper, for ornaments and cut into pieces to pass for money.

Μελίεφθα χαλκᾶ—Copper fused with honey : for

(6, 7) From this bay the coast of the gulf, according to our author, has a more easterly direction to the Straits, the distance to which from Adouli is stated at 4,000 stadia, an estimate much too liberal. In all this extent of coast the *Periplûs* mentions only the bay of the Opsianstones and conducts us at once from thence to Aunlites at the straits. Strabo however, and Juba, and Pliny, and Ptolemy mention several places in this tract, such as A r s i n o ë, B e r e-

culinary vessels and cutting into bracelets and anklets worn by certain classes of women.

Σίδηρος—Iron. Consumed in making spearheads for hunting the elephant and other animals and in making weapons of war.

Πελύκια—Hatchets.

Σκέπαρνα—Adzes.

Μάχαιραι—Swords.

Ποτήρια χαλκᾶ στρογγύλα μεγάλα—Drinking vessels of brass, large and round.

Δηνάριον ὀλίγον—A small quantity of denarii: for the use of merchants resident in the country.

Οἶνος Λαοδικηνὸς καὶ Ἰταλικὸς οὗ πολὺς—Wine, Laodikean, i.e. Syrian, from Laodike, (now Latakia) and Italian, but not much.

Ἔλαιον οὐ πολύ—Oil, but not much.

Ἀργυρώματα καὶ χρυσώματα τοπικῷ ῥυθμῷ κατεσκευασμέναι—Gold and silver plate made according to the fashion of the country for the king.

Ἀβόλλαι—Cloaks for riding or for the camp.

Καυνάκαι ἁπλοῖ—Dresses simply made of skins with the hair or fur on. These two articles of dress are not of much value.

---

nîkê, Epideirês, the Grove of Eumenês, the Chase of Puthangelos, the Territory of the Elephantophagoi, &c. The straits are called by Ptolemy Deirê or Dêrê (i. e. the neck), a word which from its resemblance in sound to the Latin *Dirae* has sometimes been explained to mean "the terrible." (I. xv. 11; IV. vii. 9; VIII. xvi. 12). "The *Periplús*," Vincent remarks, "makes no mention of Deirê, but observes that the point of contraction is close to Abalitês

These articles are imported from the interior
parts of Ariakê:—

Σίδηρος Ἰνδικὸς—Indian iron.

Στόμωμα—Sharp blades.

Ὀθόνιον Ἰνδικὸν τὸ πλατύτερον, ἡ λεγομένη μοναχή.
—Monakhê,[17] Indian cotton cloth of great width.

Σαγματογῆναι—Cotton for stuffing.

Περιζώματα— Sashes or girdles.

Καυνάκαι—Dresses of skin with the hair or fur on.

Μολόχινα—Webs of cloth mallow-tinted.

Σινδόνες ὀλίγαι—Fine muslins in small quantity.

Λάκκος χρωμάτινος—Gum-lac: yielding Lake.

The articles locally produced for export are
ivory, tortoise-shell, and rhinoceros. Most of
the goods which supply the market arrive any
time from January to September—that is, from
Tybi to Thôth. The best season, however, for
ships from Egypt to put in here is about the
month of September.

---

or the Abalìtik mart; it is from this mart that
the coast of Africa falling down first to the South
and curving afterwards towards the East is styled
the Bay of A u a l i t ê s by Ptolemy, (IV. vii.
10, 20, 27, 30, 39,) but in the *Periplûs* this name
is confined to a bay immediately beyond the
straits which D'Anville has likewise inserted in
his map, but which I did not fully understand
till I obtained Captain Cook's chart and found it
perfectly consistent with the *Periplûs*." It is the
gulf of Tejureh or Zeyla.

---

[17] Bruce, *Travels*, vol. III., p. 62.—J. B.

7. From this bay the Arabian Gulf trends eastward, and at A u a l i t ê s is contracted to its narrowest. At a distance of about 4000 stadia (*from Adouli*), if you still sail along the same coast, you reach other marts of B a r b a r i a, called the marts beyond (*the Straits*), which occur in successive order, and which, though harbourless, afford at certain seasons of the year good and safe anchorage. The first district you come to is that called A u a l i t ê s, where the passage across the strait to the opposite point of Arabia is shortest. Here is a small port of trade, called, like the district, A u a l i t ê s, which can be approached only by little boats and rafts. The imports of this place are—

'Υαλὴ λίθια σύμμικτος—Flint glass of various sorts.

[Χυλός] Διοσπολιτικῆς ὄμφακος—Juice of the sour grape of Diospolis.

The tract of country extending from the Straits to Cape Arômata (now Guardafui) is called at the present day A d e l. It is described by Strabo (XVI. iv. 14), who copies his account of it from Artemidoros. He mentions no emporium, nor any of the names which occur in the *Periplûs* except the haven of Daphnous. [Bandar Mariyah, lat. 11° 46′ N., long. 50° 38′ E.] He supplies however many particulars regarding the region which are left unnoticed by our author as having no reference to commerce—particulars, however, which prove that these parts which were resorted to in the times of the Ptolemies for elephant-hunt-

Ἱμάτια βαρβαρικὰ σύμμικτα γεγναμμένα—Cloths of different kinds worn in Barbaria dressed by the fuller.

Σῖτος—Corn.

Οἶνος—Wine.

Κασσίτερος ὀλίγος—A little tin.

The exports, which are sometimes conveyed on rafts across the straits by the B e r b e r s themselves to O k ê l i s and M o u z a on the opposite coast, are—

Ἀρώματα—Odoriferous gums.

Ἐλέφας ᾽ολίγος--Ivory in small quantity.

Χελώνη—Tortoise-shell.

Σμύρνα ἐλαχίστη διαφέρουσα δὲ τῆς ἄλλης—Myrrh in very small quantity, but of the finest sort.

Μάκειρ—Macer.

The barbarians forming the population of the place are *rude and* lawless men.

---

ing were much better known to the ancients than they were till quite recently known to ourselves. Ptolemy gives nearly the same series of names (IV. vii. 9, 10) as the *Periplús*, but with some discrepancies in the matter of their distances which he does not so accurately state. His list is: D ê r e, a city; A b a l i t ê s or Aualitês, a mart; M a l a ô, a mart; M o u n d o u or M o n d o u, a mart; Mondou, an island; Mosulon, a cape and a mart; K o b ê, a mart; E l e p h a s, a mountain; A k-k a n a i or Akannai, a mart; A r o m a t a, a cape and a mart.

The mart of A b a l i t ê s is represented by the modern Z e y l a [lat. 11° 22′ N., long. 43° 29′ E.,

8. Beyond Aualitês there is another mart,
superior to it, called M a l a ô, at a distance
by sea of 800 stadia. The anchorage is an
open road, sheltered, however, by a cape protrud-
ing eastward. The people are of a more peace-
able disposition than their neighbours. The
imports are such as have been already specified,
with the addition of—

Πλείονες χιτῶνες—Tunics in great quantity.

Σάγοι Ἀρσινοητικοὶ γεγναμμένοι καὶ βεβαμμένοι—
Coarse cloaks (or blankets) manufactured at Arsinoê, prepared by the fuller and dyed.

Μελίεφθα ὀλίγα.—A few utensils made of copper
fused with honey.

Σίδηρος—Iron.

Δηνάριον οὐ πολὺ χρυσοῦντε καὶ ἀργυροῦν—Specie,
—gold and silver, but not much.

The exports from this locality are—

Σμύρνα—Myrrh.

Λίβανος ὁ περατικὸς ὀλίγος—Frankincense *which
we call peratic, i.e.* from beyond the straits, a little
only.

---

79 miles from the straits.] On the N. shore of the
gulf are Abalit and Tejureh. Abalit is 43 miles
from the straits, and Tejureh 27 miles from
Abalit. This is the Z o u i l e h of Ebn Haukal
and the Z a l e g h of Idrisi. According to the
Periplûs it was near the straits, but Ptolemy
has fixed it more correctly at the distance from
them of 50 or 60 miles.

(8) M a l a ô as a mart was much superior to
Abalitês, from which our author estimates its
distance to be 800 stadia, though it is in reality

Κασσία σκληροτέρα—Cinnamon of a hard grain.

Δούακα—Douaka (*an inferior kind of cinnamon*).

Κάγκαμον—The gum (*for fumigation*) kangka-mon. 'Dekamalli,' gum.

Μάκειρ—The spice *macer*, which is carried to Arabia.

Σώματα σπανίως—Slaves, a few.

9.   Distant from M a l a ô a two days' sail is the trading .port of M o u n d o u, where ships find a safer anchorage by mooring at an island which lies very close to shore. The exports and imports are similar to those of the preceding marts, with the addition of the fragrant gum called *Mokrotou*, a peculiar product of the place. The native traders here are uncivilized in their manners.

10.   After M o u n d o u, if you sail eastward as before for two or three days, there comes

---

greater.   From the description he gives of its situation it must be identified with Berbereh [lat. 10° 25′ N., long. 45° 1′ E.] now the most considerable mart on this part of the coast. Vincent erroneously places it between Zeyla and the straits.

(9)   The next mart after Malaô is M o u n d o u, which, as we learn from Ptolemy, was also the name of an adjacent island—that which is now called Meyet or Burnt-island [lat. 11° 12′ N., long. 47° 17′ E., 10 miles east of Bandar Jedid].

(10)   At a distance beyond it of two or three days' sail occurs M o s u l o n, which is the name both of a mart and of a promontory. It is mentioned

next M o s u l l o n, where it is difficult to anchor.
It imports the same sorts of commodities as
have been already mentioned, and also utensils
of silver and others of iron but not so many,
and glass-ware. It exports a vast amount
of cinnamon (whence it is a port requiring
ships of heavy burden) and other fragrant
and aromatic products, besides tortoise shell,
but in no great quantity, and the incense
called *mokrotou* inferior to that of Moundou, and
frankincense brought from parts further dis-

---

by Pliny (VI. 34), who says : "Further on is the
bay of A b a l i t ê s, the island of D i o d ô r u s
and other islands which are desert. On the mainland, which has also deserts, occur a town G a z a
[Bandar Gazim, long. 49° 13′ E.], the promontory
and port of M o s y l o n, whence cinnamon is
exported. Sesostris led his army to this point
and no further. Some writers place one town of
Ethiopia beyond it, Baricaza, which lies on the
coast. According to Juba the Atlantic Sea
begins at the promontory of Mossylon." Juba
evidently confounded this promontory with Cape
Arômata, and Ptolemy, perhaps in consequence,
makes its projection more considerable than it is.
D'Anville and Gosselin thought M o s s u l o n
was situated near the promontory Mete, where
is a river, called the Soal, which they supposed
preserved traces of the name of Mossulon. This
position however cannot be reconciled with the
distances given in the *Periplûs*, which would lead
us to look for it where Guesele is placed in the

h

tant, and ivory and myrrh though in small
quantity.

11. After leaving M o s u l l o n, and sailing
past a place called N e i l o p t o l e m a i o s, and
past T a p a t ê g ê and the Little Laurel-grove,
you are conducted in two days to Cape E l e-

---

latest description given of this coast. Vincent on
very inadequate grounds would identify it with
Barbara or Berbera. [Müller places it at Bandar
Barthe and Ras Antarah, long. 49° 35′ E.]

(11) After Mosulon occurs Cape Elephant,
at some distance beyond N e i l o p t o l e m a i o s,
T a p a t e g ê, and the Little Laurel-grove. At the
Cape is a river and the Great Laurel-grove called
A k a n n a i. Strabo in his account of this coast
mentions a Neilospotamia which however can
hardly be referred to this particular locality
which pertains to the region through which the
Khori or San Pedro flows, of which Idrisi (I. 45)
thus writes : "At two journeys' distance from
Markah in the desert is a river which is subject
to risings like the Nile and on the banks of which
they sow dhorra." Regarding Cape Elephant
Vincent says, "it is formed by a mountain conspicuous in the Portuguese charts under the name
of Mount Felix or Felles from the native term
Jibel Fîl, literally, Mount Elephant. The cape
[Ras Filik, 800 ft. high, lat. 11° 57′ N., long. 50°
37′ E.] is formed by the land jutting up to the
North from the direction of the coast which is
nearly East and West, and from its northern-
most point the land falls off again South-East to
Râs 'Asir—Cape Guardafun, the Arômata of the

p h a n t. Here is a stream called E l e p h a n t
River, and tho Great Laurel-grove called A k au-
n a i, where, and where only, is produced the
peratic frankincense. The supply is most abundant, and it is of the very finest quality.

12. After this, the coast now inclining to the
south, succeeds the mart of A r ô m a t a, and a

---

ancients. We learn from Captain Saris, an English navigator, that there is a river at Jibel Fil.
In the year 1611 he stood into a bay or harbour
there which he represents as having a safe
entrance for three ships abreast : he adds also that
several sorts of gums very sweet in burning were
still purchased by the Indian ships from Cambay
which touched here for that purpose in their
passage to Mocha." The passage in the *Periplûs*
where these places are mentioned is very corrupt.
Vincent, who regards the greater D a p h n ò n
(Laurel-grove) as a river called A k a n n a i, says,
"Neither place or distance is assigned to any
of these names, but we may well allot the rivers
Daphnôn and Elephant to the synonymous town
and cape; and these may be represented by the
modern Mete and Santa Pedro." [Müller places
Elephas at Ras el Fil, long. 50° 37′ E., and Akannai at Ulûlah Bandar, long. 50° 56′ E., but they
may be represented by Ras Ahileh, where a river
enters through a lagoon in 11° 46′, and Bonah
a town with wells of good water in lat. 11° 58′ N.,
long. 50° 51′ E.]

(12) We come now to the great projection
Cape Arômata, which is a continuation of Mount
Elephant. It is called in Arabic J e r d H a f û n

bluff headland running out eastward which
forms the termination of the Barbarine coast.
The roadstead is an open one, and at certain
seasons dangerous, as the place lies exposed to

or Ras Asir; in Idrisi, C a r f o u n a, whence the
name by which it is generally known. [The South
point 11° 40′ is Râs Shenarif or Jerd Hafûn :
the N. point 11° 51′ is Râs ʼAsir.] It formed
the limit of the knowledge of this coast in the
time of Strabo, by whom it is called N o t o u
K e r a s or South Horn. It is described as a
very high bluff point and as perpendicular as if
it were scarped. [Jerd Hafûn is 2500 feet high.]
The current comes round it out of the gulf with
such violence that it is not to be stemmed without a brisk wind, and during the South-West
Monsoon, the moment you are past the Cape to
the North there is a stark calm with insufferable
heat. The current below Jerd Hafûn is noticed by
the *Periplûs* as setting to the South, and is there
perhaps equally subject to the change of the
monsoon. With this account of the coast from
the straits to the great Cape may be compared
that which has been given by Strabo, XVI. iv. 14:
" From D e i r ê the next country is that which
bears aromatic plants. The first produces myrrh
and belongs to the I c h t h y o p h a g i and
C r e o p h a g i. It bears also the persea, peach or
Egyptian almond, and the Egyptian fig. Beyond is
L i c h a, a hunting ground for elephants. There
are also in many places standing pools of rain-
water. When these are dried up, the elephants
with their trunks and tusks dig holes and find

the north wind. A coming storm gives warning
of its approach by a peculiar prognostic, for the
sea turns turbid at the bottom and changes its
colour. When this occurs, all hasten for refuge

water. On this coast there are two very large
lakes extending as far as the promontory Pytho-
laus. One of them contains salt water and is
called a sea; the other fresh water and is the
haunt of hippopotami and crocodiles. On the
margin grows the papyrus. The ibis is seen in
the neighbourhood of this place. Next is the
country which produces frankincense; it has a
promontory and a temple with a grove of poplars.
In the inland parts is a tract along the banks of a
river bearing the name of I s i s, and another that
of N i l u s, both of which produce myrrh and frankincense. Also a lagoon filled with water from the
mountains. Next the watch-post of the Lion and
the port of P y t h a n g e l u s. The next tract
bears the false cassia. There are many tracts
in succession on the sides of rivers on which
frankincense grows, and rivers extending to the
cinnamon country. The river which bounds this
tract produces rushes (φλους) in great abundance.
Then follows another river and the port of
D a p h n u s, and a valley called A p o l l o's which
bears besides frankincense, myrrh and cinnamon.
The latter is more abundant in places far in the
interior. Next is the mountain E l e p h a s, a
mountain projecting into the sea and a creek; then
follows the large harbour of P s y g m u s, a water-
ing place called that of C y n o c e p h a l i and the
last promontory of this coast N o t u-c e r a s (or the

62

to the great promontory called Tabai, which affords a secure shelter. The imports into this mart are such as have been already mentioned; while its products are cinnamon, gizeir (*a finer sort of cinnamon*), asuphê (*an ordinary sort*),

Southern Horn). After doubling this cape towards the south we have no more descriptions of harbours or places because nothing is known of the sea-coast beyond this point." [Bohn's *Transl.*] According to Gosselin, the Southern Horn corresponds with the Southern Cape of Bandel-caus, where commences the desert coast of Ajan, the ancient Azania.

According to the *Periplûs* Cape Arômata marked the termination of Barbaria and the beginning of Azania. Ptolemy however distinguishes them differently, defining the former as the interior and the latter as the sea-board of the region to which these names were applied.

The description of the Eastern Coast of Africa which now follows is carried, as has been already noticed, as far as Rhapta, a place about 6 degrees South of the Equator, but which Vincent places much farther South, identifying it with Kilwa.

The places named on this line of coast are: a promontory called Tabai, a Khersonesos; Opône, a mart; the Little and the Great Apokopa; the Little and the Great Coast; the Dromoi or courses of Azania (first that of Serapiôn, then that of Nikôn); a number of rivers; a succession of anchorages, seven in number; the Paralaoi islands; a strait or canal; the island of Menouthias; and then Rhapta,

fragrant gums, magla, motô (*an inferior cinna-mon*), and frankincense.

13. If, on sailing from T a b a i, you follow the coast of the peninsula *formed by the promontory*, you are carried by the force of a strong current to another mart 400 stadia distant, called O p ô n ê, which imports the commodities already mentioned, but produces most abundantly cin-

---

beyond which, as the author conceived, the ocean curved round Africa until it met and amalgamated with the Hesperian or Western Ocean.

(13) Tabai, to which the inhabitants of the Great Cape fled for refuge on the approach of a storm, cannot, as Vincent and others have supposed, be Cape Orfui, for it lay at too great a distance for the purpose. The projection is meant which the Arabs call Banna. [Or, Tabai may be identified with Râs Shenarif, lat. 11° 40′ N.] Tabai, Müller suggests, may be a corruption for Tabannai.

"From the foreign term Banna," he says, "certain Greeks in the manner of their countrymen invented P a n o s or P a n ô n or Panô or Panôna Kômê. Thus in Ptolemy (I. 17 and IV. 7) after Arômata follows P a n ô n K ô m ê, which Mannert has identified with Benna. [Khor Banneh is a salt lake, with a village, inside Râs Ali Beshgêl, lat. 11° 9′ N., long. 51° 9′ E.] Stephen of Byzantium may be compared, who speaks of P a n o s as a village on the Red Sea which is also called P a n ô n." The conjecture, therefore, of Letronnius that P a n ô n K ô m ê derived its name from the large apes found there, called P â n e s, falls to the ground.

namon, spice, *motô*, slaves of a very superior
sort, chiefly for the Egyptian market, and tortoise-shell of small size but in large quantity
and of the finest quality known.

14. Ships set sail from Egypt for all these
ports beyond the straits about the month of
July—that is, Epiphi. The same markets are
also regularly supplied with the products of
places far beyond them—A r i a k ê and B a r u-
g a z a. These products are—

Σῖτος—Corn.

Ὄρυζα[18]—Rice.

Βούτυρον—Butter, i. e. *ghí*.

Ἔλαιον σησάμινον—Oil of sesamum.

Ὀθόνιον ἥ τε μοναχὴ καὶ ἡ σαγματογήνη—Fine

O p ô n ê was situated on the Southern shores
of what the *Periplûs* calls a Khersonese, which
can only be the projection now called R a s
H a f û n or Cape D'Orfui (lat. 10° 25′ N.).
Ptolemy (I. 17) gives the distance of O p ô n ê
from P a n ô n K ô m ê at a 6 days' journey, from
which according to the *Periplûs* it was only
400 stadia distant. That the text of Ptolemy is
here corrupt cannot be doubted, for in his tables
the distance between the two places is not far from
that which is given in the *Periplûs*. Probably,
as Müller conjectures, he wrote ὁδόν ἡμέρας (a day's
journey) which was converted into ὁδόν ἡμερ. ϛ́ (a
six-days' journey).

(14) At this harbour is introduced the mention
of the voyage which was annually made between

---

[18] From the Tamil *ariśi*, rice deprived of the husk.—
Caldwell.

cotton called *Monakhê*, and a coarse kind for
stuffing called *Sagmatogene.*

Περιζώματα—Sashes or girdles.

Μέλι τὸ καλάμινον τὸ λεγόμενον σάκχαρι.—The
honey of a reed, called *sugar.*

Some traders undertake voyages for this
commerce expressly, while others, as they sail
along the coast *we are describing*, exchange
their cargoes for such others as they can procure.
There is no king who reigns paramount over all
this region, but each separate seat of trade is
ruled by an independent despot of its own.

15. After O p ô n ê, the coast now trending
more to the south, you come first to what are
called the little and the great A p o k o p a (or
Bluffs) of 'A z a n i a, where there are no har-

---

the coast of India and Africa in days previous to
the appearance of the Greeks on the Indian Ocean,
which has already been referred to.

(15) After leaving O p ô n ê the coast first runs
due south, then bends to the south-west, and here
begins the coast which is called the Little and the
Great A p o k o p a or Bluffs of A z a n i a, the
voyage along which occupies six days. This rocky
coast, as we learn from recent explorations, begins
at R â s M a b b e r [about lat. 9° 25′ N.], which is
between 70 and 80 miles distant from Ras Hafûn and
extends only to R â s-u l-K h e i l [about lat. 7° 45′
N.], which is distant from Râs Mabber about 140
miles or a voyage of three or four days only. The
length of this rocky coast (called H a z i n e by the
Arabs) is therefore much exaggerated in the *Peri-*

i

bours, but only roads in which ships can conveniently anchor. The navigation of this coast,
the direction of which is now to the south-
west, occupies six days. Then follow the Little
Coast and the Great Coast, occupying other six
days, when in due order succeed the D r o m o i

plûs. From this error we may infer that our author,
who was a very careful observer, had not personally
visited this coast. Ptolemy, in opposition to Marinos as well as the *Periplûs*, recognizes but one
A p o k o p a, which he speaks of as a bay. Müller
concludes an elaborate note regarding the A p o-
k o p a by the following quotation from the work of
Owen, who made the exploration already referred to,
" It is strange that the descriptive term H a z i n e
should have produced the names A j a n, A z a n
and A z a n i a in many maps and charts, as the
country never had any other appellation than
B a r r a S o m â l i or the land of the S o m â l i,
a people who have never yet been collected under
one government, and whose limits of subjection
are only within bow-shot of individual chiefs.
The coast of Africa from the Red Sea to the river
Juba is inhabited by the tribe called S o m â l i.
They are a mild people of pastoral habits and
confined entirely to the coast; the whole of the
interior being occupied by an untameable tribe of
savages called G a l l a."
The coast which follows the A p o k o p a, called
the Little and the Great A i g i a l o s or Coast,
is so desolate that, as Vincent remarks, not a
name occurs on it, neither is there an anchorage
noticed, nor the least trace of commerce to be

(or Courses) of A z a n i a, the one going
by the name of S a r a p i ô n, and the other
by that of N i k ô n. Proceeding thence, you
pass the mouths of numerous rivers, and a succession of other roadsteads lying apart one
from another a day's distance either by sea or by

---

found. Yet it is of great extent—a six days'
voyage according to the *Periplûs*, but, according
to Ptolemy, who is here more correct, a voyage of
eight days, for, as we have seen, the *Periplûs* has
unduly extended the A p o k o p a to the South.
Next follow the D r o m o i or Courses of
A z a n i a, the first called that of S e r a p i ô n
and the other that of N i k ô n. Ptolemy interposes a bay between the Great Coast and the port
of S e r a p i ô n, on which he states there was
an emporium called E s s i n a—a day's sail distant from that port. Essina, it would therefore
appear, must have been somewhere near where
M a k d a s h û [Magadoxo, lat. 2° 3′ N.] was built
by the Arabs somewhere in the eighth century A.D.
The station called that of N i k ô n in the *Periplûs*
appears in Ptolemy as the mart of T o n i k ê.
These names are not, as some have supposed, of
Greek origin, but distortions of the native appel-
lations of the places into names familiar to Greek
ears. That the Greeks had founded any settle-
ments here is altogether improbable. At the
time when the *Periplûs* was written all the trade
of these parts was in the hands of the Arabs of
M o u z a. The port of S e r a p i ô n may be
placed at a promontory which occurs in 1° 40′
of N. lat. From this, T o n i k ê, according to

land. There are seven of them altogether, and they reach on to the P u r a l a o i islands and the *narrow strait* called the Canal, beyond which, where the coast changes its direction from south-west slightly more to south, you are conducted by a voyage of two days and two nights to M e-

---

the tables of Ptolemy, was distant 45', and its position must therefore have agreed with that of T o r r e or Torra of our modern maps.

Next occurs a succession of rivers and road-steads, seven in number, which being passed we are conducted to the P u r a l a ä n Islands, and what is called a canal or channel (διώρυξ). These islands are not mentioned elsewhere. They can readily be identified with the two called M a n d a and L a m o u, which are situate at the mouths of large rivers, and are separated from the mainland and from each other by a narrow channel. Vincent would assign a Greek origin to the name of these islands. "With a very slight alteration," he says, "of the reading, the Puralian Islands (Πῦρ ἅλιον, *marine fire*,) are the islands of the Fiery Ocean, and nothing seems more consonant to reason than for a Greek to apply the name of the Fiery Ocean to a spot which was the centre of the Torrid Zone and subject to the perpendicular rays of an equinoctial sun." [The Juba islands run along the coast from Juba to about Lat. 1° 50′ S., and Manda bay and island is in Lat. 2° 12′ S.]

Beyond these islands occurs, after a voyage of two days and two nights, the island of M e-nouthias or Menouthesias, which it has

nouthias, an island stretching towards sunset,
and distant from the mainland about 300 stadia.
It is low-lying and woody, has rivers, and a
vast variety of birds, and yields the mountain
tortoise, but it has no wild beasts at all, except
only crocodiles, which, however, are quite

---

been found difficult to identify with any certainty.
"It is," says Vincent, "the *Eitenediommenouthesias*
of the *Periplûs*, a term egregiously strange and
corrupted, but out of which the commentators
unanimously collect Menoothias, whatever may be
the fate of the remaining syllables. That this Menoothias," he continues, "must have been one of
the Zangibar islands is indubitable; for the distance from the coast of all three, Pemba, Zangibar,
and Momfia, affords a character which is indelible;
a character applicable to no other island from
Guardafui to Madagascar." He then identifies
it with the island of Zangibar, lat. 6° 5′ S., in preference to Pemba, 5° 6′ S., which lay too far out
of the course, and in preference to Momfia, 7° 50′
S. (though more doubtfully), because of its being
by no means conspicuous, whereas Zangibar was
so prominent and obvious above the other two,
that it might well attract the particular attention
of navigators, and its distance from the mainland
is at the same time so nearly in accordance with
that given in the *Periplûs* as to counterbalance all
other objections. A writer in Smith's *Classical
Geography*, who seems to have overlooked the indications of the distances both of Ptolemy and the
Periplûs, assigns it a position much further to the
north than is reconcilable with these distances.

harmless. The boats are here made of planks sewn together attached to a keel formed of a single log of wood, and these are used for fishing and for catching turtle. This is also caught in another mode, peculiar to the island, by lowering wicker-baskets instead of nets, and fixing

---

He places it about a degree south from the mouth of the River Juba or Govind, just where an opening in the coral-reefs is now found. " The coasting voyage," he says, " steering S. W., reached the island on the east side—a proof that it was close to the main. . . . It is true the navigator says it was 300 stadia from the mainland ; but as there is no reason to suppose that he surveyed the island, this distance must be taken to signify the estimated width of the northern inlet separating the island from the main, and this estimate is probably much exaggerated. The mode of fishing with baskets is still practised in the Juba islands and along this coast. The formation of the coast of E. Africa in these latitudes—where the hills or downs upon the coast are all formed of a coral conglomerate comprising fragments of madrepore, shell and sand, renders it likely that the island which was close to the main 16 or 17 centuries ago, should now be united to it. Granting this theory of gradual transformation of the coast-line, the M e n o u t h i a s of the *Periplûs* may be supposed to have stood in what is now the rich garden-land of S h a m b a, where the rivers carrying down mud to mingle with the marine deposit of coral drift covered the choked-up estuary with a rich soil."

them against the mouths of the cavernous
rocks which lie out in the sea confronting the
beach.

16. At the distance of a two days' sail from
this island lies the last of the marts of A z a n i a,
called R h a p t a, a name which it derives
from the sewn boats just mentioned. Ivory is
procured here in the greatest abundance, and
also turtle. The indigenous inhabitants are

The island is said in the *Periplûs* to extend
towards the West, but this does not hold good
either in the case of Zangibar or any other island
in this part of the coast. Indeed there is no one
of them in which at the present day all the
characteristics of M e n o u t h i a s are found combined. M o m fi a, for instance, which resembles
it somewhat in name, and which, as modern
travellers tell us, is almost entirely occupied with
birds and covered with their dung, does not
possess any streams of water These are found
in Zangibar. The author may perhaps have con-
fusedly blended together the accounts he had
received from his Arab informants.

(16) We arrive next and finally at R h a p t a, the
last emporium on the coast known to the author.
Ptolemy mentions not only a city of this name,
but also a river and a promontory. The name
is Greek (from ῥάπτειν, *to sew*), and was applied
to the place because the vessels there in use
were raised from bottoms consisting of single
trunks of trees by the addition of planks which
were sewn together with the fibres of the cocoa.

men of huge stature, who live *apart from each other*, every man ruling like a lord his own domain. The whole territory is governed by the despot of M o p h a r i t i s, because the sovereignty over it, by some right of old standing, is vested in the kingdom of what is called the First Arabia. The merchants of M o u z a farm its revenues from the king, and employ in trading with it a great many ships of heavy burden, on board of which they have Arabian command- ers and factors who are intimately acquainted with the natives and have contracted marriage

---

" It is a singular fact," as Vincent remarks, "that this peculiarity should be one of the first objects which attracted the attention of the Portuguese upon their reaching this coast. They saw them first at Mozambique, where they were called *Almeidas*, but the principal notice of them in most of their writers is generally stated at Kilwa, the very spot which we have supposed to receive its name from vessels of the same con- struction." Vincent has been led from this coinci- dence to identify Rhapta with Kilwa [lat. 8° 50′ S.]. Müller however would place it not so far south, but somewhere in the Bay of Zangibar. The promontory of R h a p t u m, he judges from the indications of the *Periplûs* to be the projection which closes the bay in which lies the island of Zangibar, and which is now known as M o i n a n o- k a l û or Point Pouna, lat. 7° S. The parts beyond this were unknown, and the southern coast of Africa, it was accordingly thought by the ancient

with them, and know their language and the navigation of the coast.

17. The articles imported into these marts are principally javelins manufactured at Mouza, hatchets, knives, awls, and crown glass of various sorts, to which must be added corn and wine in no small quantity landed at particular ports, not for sale, but to entertain and thereby conciliate the barbarians. The articles which these places export are ivory, in great abundance but of inferior quality to that obtained at Adouli, rhinoceros, and tortoise-shell of fine quality, second only to the Indian, and a little *nauplius*.

---

geographers, began here. Another cape however is mentioned by Ptolemy remoter than Rhaptum and called Prasum (that is the Green Cape) which may perhaps be Cape Delgado, which is noted for its luxuriant vegetation. The same author calls the people of Rhapta, the Rhapsioi Aithiopes. They are described in the *Periplûs* as men of lofty stature, and this is still a characteristic of the Africans of this coast. The Rhapsii were, in the days of our author, subject to the people of Mouza in Arabia just as their descendants are at the present day subject to the Sultan of Maskat. Their commerce moreover still maintains its ancient characteristics. It is the African who still builds and mans the ships while the Arab is the navigator and supercargo. The ivory is still of inferior quality, and the turtle is still captured at certain parts of the coast.

j

18. These marts, we may say, are about the last on the coast of A z a n i a—the coast, that is, which is on your right as you sail *south* from B e r e n i k ê. For beyond these parts an ocean, hitherto unexplored, curves round towards sunset, and, stretching along the southern extremities of Ethiopia, Libya, and Africa, amalgamates with the Western Sea.

19. To the left, again, of B e r e n i k ê, if you

(18, 19) Our author having thus described the African coast as far southward as it was known on its Eastern side, reverts to B e r e n i k ê and enters at once on a narrative of the second voyage—that which was made thence across the Northern head of the gulf and along the coast of Arabia to the emporium of M o u z a near the Straits. The course is first northward, and the parts about B e r e n i k ê as you bear away lie therefore now on your left hand. Having touched at M y o s H o r m o s the course on leaving it is shaped eastward across the gulf by the promontory P h a r a n, and L e u k ê K ô m ê[19] is reached after three or four days' sailing. This was a port in the kingdom of the Nabathæans (the Nebaioth of Scripture), situated perhaps near the mouth of the Elanitic Gulf or eastern arm of the Red Sea, now called the Gulf of Akabah. Much difference of opinion has prevailed as to its exact position, since the encroachment of the land upon the sea has much altered the line of coast here. Mannert identified it with the modern Y e n b o [lat. 24° 5′ N., long. 38′ 3′ E., the port

[19] Meaning *white village.*

sail eastward from M y o s-H o r m o s across the
adjacent gulf for two days, or perhaps three, you
arrive at a place having a port and a fortress
which is called L e u k ê K ô m ê, and forming the
point of communication with Petra, the residence
of M a l i k h a s, the king of the Nabatæans. It
ranks as an emporium of trade, since small
vessels come to it laden with merchandize from
Arabia; and hence an officer is deputed to

---

of Medina], Gosselin with M o w i l a h [lat. 27°
38′ N., long. 35° 28′ E.,] Vincent with E y n o u n a h
[lat. 28° 3′ N., long. 35° 13′ E.—the O n n e of
Ptolemy], Reichhard with I s t a b e l A n t a i, and
Rüppel with W e j h [lat. 26° 13′ N., long. 36°
27′ E]. Müller prefers the opinion held by Bochart,
D'Anville, Quatremère, Noel des Vergers, and
Ritter, who agree in placing it at the port called
H a u a r a [lat. 24° 59′ N., long. 37° 16′ E.) mentioned by Idrisi (I. p. 332), who describes it as a
village inhabited by merchants carrying on a considerable trade in earthen vases manufactured at
a clay-pit in their neighbourhood. Near it lies
the island of H a s s a n i [lat. 24° 59′ N., long.
37° 3′ E.], which, as Wellsted reports, is conspicuous from its *white* appearance. L e u k ê
K ô m ê is mentioned by various ancient authors,
as for instance Strabo, who, in a passage wherein he recounts the misfortunes which befel the
expedition which Aelius led into Nabathaea,
speaks of the place as a large mart to which and
from which the camel traders travel with ease
and in safety from P e t r a and back to P e t r a

collect the duties which are levied on imports 'at the rate of twenty-five per cent. of their value, and also a centurion who commands the garrison by which the place is protected.

20. Beyond this mart, and quite contiguous to it, is the realm of Arabia, which stretches to a great distance along the coast of the Red Sea. It is inhabited by various tribes, some speaking the same language with a certain degree of

---

with so large a body of men and camels as to differ in no respect from an army.

The merchandize thus conveyed from L e u k ê K ô m ê to P e t r a was passed on to R h i- n o k o l o u r a in Palestine near Egypt, and thence to other nations, but in his own time the greater part was transported by the Nile to A l e x a n d r i a. It was brought down from India and Arabia to M y o s H o r m o s, whence it was first conveyed on camels to K o p t o s and thence by the Nile to A l e x a n d r i a. The Nabathaean king, at the time when our author visited L e u k ê K ô m ê, was, as he tells us, M a l i k h a s, a name which means ' king.' Two Petraean sovereigns so called are mentioned by Josêphos, of whom the latter was contemporary with Herod. The Malikhas of the *Periplûs* is however not mentioned in any other work. The Nabathaean kingdom was subverted in the time of Trajan, A.D. 105, as we learn from Dio Cassius (cap. lxviii. 14), and from Eutropius (viii. 2, 9), and from Ammianus Marcellinus (xiv. 8).

(20) At no great distance from L e u k ê K ô m ê the Nabathaean realm terminates and Arabia

77

uniformity, and others a language totally different. Here also, *as on the opposite continent*, the
sea-board is occupied by I k h t h y o p h a g o i,
who live in dispersed huts ; while the men of the
interior live either in villages, or where pasture
can be found, and are an evil race of men,
speaking two different languages. If a vessel
is driven from her course upon this shore she
is plundered, and if wrecked the crew on
escaping to land are reduced to slavery. For
this reason they are treated as enemies and captured by the chiefs and kings of Arabia. They
are called K a n r a i t a i. Altogether, therefore,
the navigation of this part of the Arabian coast
is very dangerous : for, *apart from the barbarity
of its people*, it has neither harbours nor good
roadsteads, and it is foul with breakers, and
girdled with rocks which render it inaccessible.
For this reason when sailing south we stand off

---

begins. The coast is here described as most dismal, and as in every way dangerous to navigation.
The inhabitants at the same time are barbarians,
destitute of all humanity, who scruple not to
attack and plunder wrecked ships and to make
slaves of their crews if they escaped to land. The
mariner therefore, shunned these inhospitable
shores, and standing well out to sea, sailed down
the middle of the gulf. The tribe here spoken of
was that perhaps which is represented by the
H u t e m i of the present day, and the coast belonged to the part of Arabia now called H e j i d.

from a shore in every way so dreadful, and
keep our course down the middle of the gulf,
straining our utmost to reach *the more civilized
part* of Arabia, which begins at Burnt Island.
From this onward the people are under a regular government, and, as their country is pastoral,
they keep herds of cattle and camels.

21. Beyond this tract, and on the shore of a
bay which occurs at the termination of the left
(or east) side of the gulf, is M o u z a, an established and notable mart of trade, at a distance

---

A more civilized region begins at an island
called Burnt island, which answers to the modern
Zebâyir [about lat. 15° 5′ N., long. 42° 12′ E.],
an island which was till recently volcanic.

(21) Beyond this is the great emporium called
M o u z a, [lat. 13°43′ N., long. 43° 5′ 14″ E.] situated
in a bay near the termination of the Gulf, and at a
distance from B e r e n i k ê of 12,000 stadia. Here
the population consists almost entirely of merchants
and mariners, and the place is in the highest degree
commercial. The commodities of the country are
rich and numerous (though this is denied by
Pliny), and there is a great traffic in Indian
articles brought from B a r u g a z a (Bharoch).
This port, once the most celebrated and most frequented in Yemen, is now the village Musa about
twenty-five miles north from Mokhâ, which has
replaced it as a port, the foundation of which dates
back no more than 400 years ago. " Twenty miles
inland from Mokhâ," says Vincent, " Niebuhr discovered a Musa still existing, which he with great

south from Berenikê of not more than 12,000
stadia. The whole place is full of Arabian ship-
masters and common sailors, and is absorbed
in the pursuits of commerce, for with ships of its
own fitting out, it trades with the marts beyond
the Straits on the opposite coast, and also with
B a r u g a z a.

22. Above this a three days' journey off lies the
city of S a u ê, in the district called M o p h a-
r i t i s. It is the residence of K h o l a i b o s, the
despot of that country.

---

probability supposes to be the ancient mart now
carried inland to this distance by the recession of
the coast." [He must have confounded it with
J e b e l M u s a, due east of Mokhâ, at the commencement of the mountain country.] It is a
mere village badly built. Its water is good, and
is said to be drunk by the wealthier inhabitants
of Mokhâ. Bochart identified M o u z a with the
M e s h a mentioned by Moses.

(22) The *Periplûs* notices two cities that lay
inland from M o u z a—the 1st S a u ê, the S a v ê
of Pliny (VI. xxvi., 104), and also of Ptolemy
(VI. vii., p. 411), who places it at a distance of
500 stadia S. E. of M o u z a. The position and
distance direct us to the city of T a a e s, which lies
near a mountain called S a b e r. S a u ê belonged to a
district called M a p h a r i t i s or M o p h a r e i t ê s,
a name which appears to survive in the modern
M h a r r a s, which designates a mountain lying
N. E. from T a a e s. It was ruled by K h o l a i b o s
(Arabicé—Khaleb), whom our author calls a tyrant,

23. A journey of nine days more conducts us to S a p h a r, the metropolis of K h a r i b a ê l, the rightful sovereign of two contiguous tribes, the H o m ê r i t e s and the S a b a ï t a j, and, by means of frequent embassies and presents, the friend of the Emperors.

---

and who was therefore probably a Sheikh who had revolted from his lawful chief, and established himself as an independent ruler.

(23) The other city was S a p h a r, the metropolis of the H o m e r î t a i, *i.e.* the H i m a r y i—the Arabs of Yemen, whose power was widely extended, not only in Yemen but in distant countries both to the East and West. Saphar is called S a p p h a r by Ptolemy (VI. vii.), who places it in 14° N. lat. Philostorgios calls it T a p h a r o n, and Stephen of Byzantium T a r p h a r a. It is now D h a f a r or Dsoffar or Zaphar. In Edrisi (I. p. 148) it appears as D h o f a r, and he thus writes of it :—" It is the capital of the district Jahsseb. It was formerly one of the greatest and most famous of cities. The kings of Yemen made it their residence, and there was to be seen the palace of Zeidan. These structures are now in ruins, and the population has been much decreased, nevertheless the inhabitants have preserved some remnants of their ancient riches." The ruins of the city and palace still exist in the neighbourhood of J e r i m, which Niebuhr places in 14° 30′ N. lat. The distance from S a u ê to S a p h a r in the *Periplûs* is a nine days' journey. Niebuhr accomplished it however in six. Perhaps, as Müller suggests, the nine days' journey is from

24. The mart of M o u z a has no harbour, but its sea is smooth, and the anchorage good, owing to the sandy nature of the bottom. The commodities which it imports are—

Πορφύρα, διάφορος καὶ χυδαία—Purple cloth, fine and ordinary.

Ἱματισμὸς Ἀραβικὸς χειριδωτὸς, ὅτε ἁπλοῦς καὶ ὁ κοινὸς καὶ σκοτουλᾶτος καὶ διάχρυσος—Garments made up in the Arabian fashion, some plain and common, and others wrought in needlework and inwoven with gold.

Κρόκος—Saffron.

Κύπερος—The aromatic rush Kyperos. (Turmeric?)

Ὀθόνιον—Muslins.

Ἀβόλλαι—Cloaks.

Λώδικες οὐ πολλαὶ, ἁπλοῖ τε καὶ ἐντόπιοι—Quilts, in small quantity, some plain, others adapted to the fashion of the country.

Ζῶναι σκιωταὶ—Sashes of various shades of colour.

Μύρον μέτριον—Perfumes, a moderate quantity.

Χρῆμα ἱκανὸν—Specie as much as is required.

Οἶνος—Wine.

Σῖτος οὐ πολύς—Corn, but not much.

M o u z a to S a p h a r. The sovereign of Saphar is called by our author K h a r i b a ê l, a name which is not found among the Himyaritic kings known from other sources. In Ptolemy the region is called E l i s a r ô n, from a king bearing that name.

(24) Adjacent to the Homeritai, and subject to them when the *Periplûs* was written, were the Sabaeans, so famous in antiquity for their wealth,

k

The country produces a little wheat and a
great abundance of wine. Both the king and
the despot above mentioned receive presents
consisting of horses, pack-saddle mules, gold
plate, silver plate embossed, robes of great value,
and utensils of brass. M o u z a exports its
own local products—myrrh of the finest quality
that has oozed in drops from the trees, both the
Gabiræan and Minœan kinds; white marble (or
alabaster), in addition to commodities brought
from the other side of the Gulf, all such as were
enumerated at A d o u l i. The most favourable
season for making a voyage to Mouza is the month
of September,—that is Thoth,—but there is
nothing to prevent it being made earlier.

25. If on proceeding from M o u z a you sail
by the coast for about a distance of 300 stadia,

---

luxury and magnificence. Their country, the
S h e b a of Scripture, was noted as the land of
frankincense. Their power at one time extended
far and wide, but in the days of our author they
were subject to the Homerites ruled over by
Kharibaêl, who was assiduous in courting the
friendship of Rome.

(25) At a distance of 300 stadia beyond M o u z a
we reach the straits where the shores of Arabia
and Africa advance so near to each other that the
passage between them has only, according to the
Periplûs, a width of 60 stadia, or 7½ miles. In the
midst of the passage lies the island of D i o-
d ô r o s (now Perim), which is about 4½ miles long
by 2 broad, and rises 230 feet above the level of the

there occurs, where the Arabian mainland and
the opposite coast of B a r b a r i a at A n a-
l i t ê s now approach each other, a channel of no
great length which contracts the sea and encloses
it within narrow bounds.   This is 60 stadia wide,
and in crossing it you come midway upon the
island of D i o d ô r o s, to which it is owing that
the passage of the straits is in its neighbourhood
exposed to violent winds which blow down
from the adjacent mountains.   There is situate
upon the shore of the straits an Arabian village
subject to the same ruler (as Mouza), O k ê l i s
by name, which is not so much a mart of commerce as a place for anchorage and supplying
water, and where those who are bound for the
interior first land and halt to refresh themselves.

---

sea.   The straits, according to Moresby, are 14½
geographical miles wide at the entrance between
Bab-el-Mandab Cape (near which is Perim) and
the opposite point or volcanic peak called J i b e l
S i j a n.   The larger of the two entrances is 11 miles
wide, and the other only 1½.   Strabo, Agathêmeros,
and Pliny all agree with the *Periplûs* in giving 60
stadia as the breadth of the straits.   The first
passage of those dreaded straits was regarded as
a great achievement, and was naturally ascribed
to Sesostris as the voyage though the straits of
Kalpê was ascribed to Heraklês.

Situated on the shores of the straits was
a place called O k ê l i s.   This was not a
mart of commerce, but merely a bay with

26. Beyond O k ê l i s, the sea again widening out towards the east, and gradually expanding into the open main, there lies, at about the distance of 1,200 stadia, E u d a i m ô n A r a b i a, a maritime village subject to that kingdom of which Kharibaêl is sovereign—a place with good anchorage, and supplied with sweeter and better water than that of Okêlis, and standing at the entrance of a bay where the land begins to

---

good anchorage and well supplied with water. It is identical with the modern Ghalla or Cella, which has a bay immediately within the straits. Strabo following Artemidoros notes here a promontory called A k i l a. Pliny (VI. xxxii. 157) mentions an emporium of the same name "ex quo in Indiam navigatur." In xxvi., 104 of the same Book he says : " Indos petentibus utilissimum est ab O c e l i egredi." Ptolemy mentions a P s e u d o k ê l i s, which he places at the distance of half a degree from the emporium of O k ê l i s.

(26) At a distance beyond O k ê l i s of 1,200 stadia is the port of E u d a i m ô n A r a b i a, which beyond doubt corresponds to 'Â d e n, [lat. 12° 45′ N., long. 45° 21′ E.] now so well-known as the great packet station between Suez and India. The opinion held by some that Aden is the Eden mentioned by the Prophet Ezekiel (xxvii. 23) is opposed by Ritter and Winer. It is not mentioned by Pliny, though it has been erroneously held that the A t t a n a e, which he mentions in the following passage, was Aden. " Homnae

retire inwards. It was called Eudaimôn ('rich
and prosperous'), because in bygone days, when
the merchants from India did not proceed
to Egypt, and those from Egypt did not venture
to cross over to the marts further east, but both
came only as far as this city, it formed the common centre of their commerce, as Alexandria
receives the wares which pass to and fro
between Egypt and the ports of the Mediter-

---

et Attanae (v. l. Athanae) quæ nunc oppida
maxime celebrari a Persico mari negotiatores
dicunt." (vi. 32.) Ptolemy, who calls it simply
A r a b i a, speaks of it as an emporium, and places
after it at the distance of a degree and a half
M e l a n H o r o s, or Black Hill, 17 miles from
the coast, which is in long. 46° 59′ E. The place,
as the *Periplûs* informs us, received the name
of E u d a i m ô n from the great prosperity and
wealth which it derived from being the great
entrepôt of the trade between India and Egypt.
It was in decay when that work was written, but
even in the time of Ptolemy had begun to show
symptoms of returning prosperity, and in the time
of Constantine it was known as the 'Roman Emporium,' and had almost regained its former consequence, as is gathered from a passage in the
works of the ecclesiastical historian Philostorgios.
It is thus spoken of by Edrisi (I. p. 51): "'À d e n
is a small town, but renowned for its seaport
whence ships depart that are destined for Sind,
India, and China." In the middle ages it became
again the centre of the trade between India and

ranean. Now, however, it lies in ruins, the Emperor having destroyed it not long before our own times.

27. To E u d a i m ô n A r a b i a at once succeeds a great length of coast and a' bay extending 2,000 stadia or more, inhabited by nomadic tribes and Ikhthyophagoi settled in villages. On doubling a cape which projects from it you come to another trading seaport, K a n ê, which

---

the Red Sea, and thus regained that wonderful prosperity which in the outset had given it its name. In this flourishing condition it was found by Marco Polo, whose account of its wealth, power and influence is, as Vincent remarks, almost as magnificent as that which Agatharkhidês attributed to the Sabæans in the time of the Ptolemies, when the trade was carried on in the same manner. Agatharkhidês does not however mention the place by name, but it was probably the city which he describes without naming it as lying on the White Sea without the straits, whence, he says, the Sabæans sent out colonies or factories into India, and where the fleets from Persis, Karmania and the Indus arrived. The name of A d e n is supposed to be a corruption from E u d a i m ô n.

(27) The coast beyond Aden is possessed partly by wandering tribes, and partly by tribes settled in villages which subsist on fish. Here occurs a bay—that now called Ghubhet-al-Kamar, which extends upwards of 2,000 stadia, and ends in a promontory—that now called Râs-al-Asîdah or

is subject to E l e a z o s, king of the incense
country. Two barren islands lie opposite to it,
120 stadia off—one called O r n e ô n, and the
other T r o u l l a s. At some distance inland
from K a n ê is S a b b a t h a, the principal city
of the district, where the king resides. At
K a n ê is collected all the incense that is produced in the country, this being conveyed to it
partly on camels, and partly *by sea* on floats

Bâ-l-hâf [lat. 13° 58′ N., long 48° 9′ S.—a cape
with a hill near the fishing village of Gillah].
Beyond this lies another great mart called K a n ê.
It is mentioned by Pliny, and also by Ptolemy,
who assigns it a position in agreement with the
indications given in the *Periplûs*. It has been
identified with the port now called Hisn Ghorâb
[lat. 14° 0′ N. long. 48° 19′ E.]. Not far from this
is an island called Halanî, which answers to the
T r o u l l a s of our author. Further south is another island, which is called by the natives of the
adjacent coast S i k k a h, but by sailors Jibûs.
This is covered with the dung of birds which in
countless multitudes have always frequented it,
and may be therefore identified with the O r n e ô n
of the *Periplûs*. K a n ê was subject to Eleazos, the
king of the Frankincense Country, who resided at
S a b b a t h a, or as it is called by Pliny (VI. xxxii.
155) S a b o t a, the capital of the Atramîtae or
Adramitae, a tribe of Sabæans from whom the
division of Arabia now known as Hadhramaut
takes its name. The position of this city cannot
be determined with certainty. Wellsted, who pro-

supported on inflated skins, a local invention, and also in boats. K a n ê carries on trade with ports across the ocean—B a r u g a z a, S k y t h i a, and O m a n a, and the adjacent coast of P e r s i s.

28.. From Egypt it imports, like Mouza, corn and a little wheat, cloths for the Arabian

---

ceeded into the interior from the coast near Hisn Ghorab through Wadi Meifah, came after a day's journey and a half to a place called Nakb-el-Hajar, situated in a highly cultivated district, where he found ruins of an ancient city of the Himyarites crowning an eminence that rose gently with a double summit from the fertile plain. The city appeared to have been built in the most solid style of architecture, and to have been protected by a very lofty wall formed of square blocks of black marble, while the inscriptions plainly betokened that it was an old seat of the Himyarites. A close similarity could be traced between its ruins and those of K a n ê, to which there was an easy communication by the valley of M e i f a h. This place, however, can hardly be regarded as S a b-b a t h a without setting aside the distances given by Ptolemy, and Wellsted moreover learned from the natives that other ruins of a city of not less size were to be met with near a village called Esan, which could be reached by a three days' journey.—(See Haines, *Mem. of the S. Coast of Arab.*)

(28) With regard to the staple product of this region—frankincense, the *Periplûs* informs us that

market, both of the common sort and the plain,
and large quantities of a sort that is adulterated;
also copper, tin, coral, styrax, and all the other
articles enumerated at Mouza. Besides these
there are brought also, principally for the king,
wrought silver plate, and specie as well as
horses and carved images, and plain cloth of
a superior quality. Its exports are its indigenous products, frankincense and aloes, and such
commodities as it shares in common with other
marts on the same coast. Ships sail for this
port at the same season of the year as those
bound for Mouza, but earlier.

29. As you proceed from K a n ê the land

---

it was brought for exportation to K a n ê. It was
however in the first place, if we may credit Pliny,
conveyed to the Metropolis. He says (xv. 32)
that when gathered it was carried into S a b o t a
on camels which could enter the city only by
one particular gate, and that to take it by any
other route was a crime punished by death. The
priests, he adds, take a tithe for a deity named
S a b i s, and that until this impost is paid, the
article cannot be sold.

Some writers would identify S a b b a t h a
with M a r i a b o (Marab), but on insufficient
grounds. It has also been conjectured that the
name may be a lengthened form of S a b a (Sheba),
a common appellation for cities in Arabia Felix.
[Müller places Sabbatha at Sawa, lat. 16° 13′ N.,
long. 48° 9′ E.]

(29) The next place mentioned by our author

l

retires more and more, and there succeeds
another very deep and far-stretching gulf,
S a k h a l i t ê s by name, and also the frankincense country, which is mountainous and
difficult of access, having a dense air loaded
with vapours [and] the frankincense exhaled
from the trees. These trees, which are not of any
great size or height, yield their incense in the
form of a concretion on the bark, just as several
of our trees in Egypt exude gum. The incense
is collected by the hand of the king's slaves, and
malefactors condemned to this service as a
punishment. The country is unhealthy in the
extreme :—pestilential even to those who sail
along the coast, and mortal to the poor wretches
who gather the incense, who also suffer from
lack of food, which readily cuts them off.

30. Now at this gulf is a promontory, the
greatest in the world, looking towards the east,

---

after K a n ê is a Bay called S a k h a l î t e s, which
terminates at S u a g r o s, a promontory which
looks eastward, and is the greatest cape in the
whole world. There was much difference of
opinion among the ancient geographers regarding
the position of this Bay, and consequently regarding that of Cape S u a g r o s.

(30) Some would identify the latter with Râs-
el-Ḥad, and others on account of the similarity
of the name with Cape S a u g r a or S a u k i r a h
[lat. 18° 8′ N., long. 56° 35′ E.], where Ptolemy
places a city S u a g r o s at a distance of 6 degrees

and called S u a g r o s, at which is a fortress which protects the country, and a harbour, and a magazine to which the frankincense which is collected is brought. Out in the open sea, facing this promontory, and lying between it and the promontory of A r ô m a t a, which projects from the opposite coast, though nearer to S u a g r o s, is the island going by the name of D i o s k o r i d ê s, which is of great extent, but

---

from K a n ê. But S u a g r o s is undoubtedly Ras Fartak [lat. 15° 39′ N., long. 52° 15′ E.], which is at a distance of 4 degrees from H i s n G h o r a b, or K a n ê, and which, rising to the height of 2,500 feet on a coast which is all low-lying, is a very conspicuous object, said to be discernible from a distance of 60 miles out at sea. Eighteen miles west from this promontory is a village called Saghar, a name which might probably have suggested to the Greeks that of S u a g r o s. Consistent with this identification is the passage of Pliny (VI. 32) where he speaks of the island D i o s c o r i d i s (Sokotra) as distant from S u a g r o s, which he calls the utmost projection of the coast, 2,240 stadia or 280 miles, which is only about 30 miles in excess of the real distance, 2,000 stadia.

With regard to the position of the Bay of Sakhalitês, Ptolemy, followed by Marcianus, places it to the East of Suagros. Marinos on the other hand, like the *Periplûs*, places it to the west of it. Müller agrees with Fresnel in regarding S a k h l ê, mentioned by Ptolemy (VI. vii. 41) as

desert and very moist, having rivers and crocodiles and a great many vipers, and lizards of
enormous size, of which the flesh serves for food,
while the grease is melted down and used as a
substitute for oil. This island does not, however, produce either the grape or corn. The
population, which is but scanty, inhabits the
north side of the island—that part of it which
looks towards the mainland (*of Arabia*). It

1½ degree East of Makalleh [lat. 14° 31' N., long
49° 7' W.] as the same with Shehr—which is now
the name of all that mountainous region extending
from the seaport of Makalleh to the bay in which
lie the islands of Kurya Murya. He therefore
takes this to be in the Regio Sakhalîtês, and
rejects the opinion of Ptolemy as inconsistent
with this determination. With regard to Shehr
or Shehar [lat. 14° 38' N., long. 49° 22' E.] Yule
(*M. Polo*, II. vol. p. 440, note) says: " Shihr or Shehr
still exists on the Arabian Coast as a town and
district about 330 miles east of Aden." The name
Shehr in some of the oriental geographies in-
cludes the whole Coast up to Oman. The hills of
the Shehr and Dhafâr districts were the great
source of produce of the Arabian frankincense.

The island of D i o s k o r i d ê s (now Sokotra)
is placed by the *Periplûs* nearer to Cápe S u a-
g r o s than to Cape A r ô m a t a—although its distance from the former is nearly double the distance
from the latter. The name, though in appearance
a Greek one, is in reality of Sanskrit origin ; from
Dvîpa Sukhâddra, i.e. *insula fortunata*, ' Island abode

consists of an intermixture of foreigners, Arabs,
Indians, and even Greeks, who resort hither for
the purposes of commerce. The island produces the tortoise,—the genuine, the land, and
the white sort: the latter very abundant, and
distinguished for the largeness of its shell; also
the mountain sort which is of extraordinary size
and has a very thick shell, whereof the under-
part cannot be used, being too hard to cut,

---

of Bliss.' The accuracy of the statements made
regarding it in the *Periplûs* is fully confirmed by
the accounts given of it by subsequent writers.
Kosmas, who wrote in the 6th century, says that
the inhabitants spoke Greek, and that he met with
people from it who were on their way to Ethiopia,
and that they spoke Greek. "The ecclesiastical
historian Nikephoros Kallistos," says Yule, "seems
to allude to the people of Sokotra when he says
that among the nations visited by the Missionary
Theophilus in the time of Constantius, were 'the
Assyrians on the verge of the outer Ocean,
towards the East . . . whom Alexander the
Great, after driving them from Syria, sent thither
to settle, and to this day they keep their
mother tongue, though all of the blackest, through
the power of the sun's rays.' The Arab voyagers
of the 9th century say that the island was
colonized with Greeks by Alexander the Great,
in order to promote the culture of the Sokotrine
aloes; when the other Greeks adopted Christianity
these did likewise, and they had continued to
retain their profession of it. The colonizing by

while the serviceable part is made into money-
boxes, tablets, escritoires, and ornamental articles
of that description. It yields also the vegetable
dye (κιννάβαρι) called Indicum (or Dragon's-
blood), which is gathered as it distils from
trees.

31. The island is subject to the king of the
frankincense country, in the same way as
A z a n i a is subject to Kharibaël and the despot
of M o p h a r i t i s. It used to be visited by
some (*merchants*) from Mouza, and others on
the homeward voyage from Limurikê and
Barugaza would occasionally touch at it, import-
ing rice, corn, Indian cotton and female-slaves,
who, being rare, always commanded a ready
market. In exchange for these commodities
they would receive as fresh cargo great quantities of tortoise-shell. The revenues of the
island are at the present day farmed out by its
sovereigns, who, however, maintain a garrison
in it for the protection of their interests.

Alexander is probably a fable, but invented to
account for facts." (*Marco Polo* II. 401.) The aloe,
it may be noted, is not mentioned in the *Periplûs* as
one of the products of the island. The islanders,
though at one time Christians, are now Muham-
madans, and subject as of yore to Arabia. The
people of the interior are still of distinct
race with curly hair, Indian complexion, and
regular features. The coast people are mongrels
of Arab and mixed descent. Probably in old times

32. Immediately after S u a g r o s follows a gulf deeply indenting the mainland of O m a n a, and having a width of 600 stadia. Beyond it are high mountains, rocky and precipitous, and inhabited by men who live in caves. The range extends onward for 500 stadia, and beyond where it terminates lies an important harbour called M o s k h a, the appointed port to

Ms. [?]

---

civilization and Greek may have been confined to the littoral foreigners. Marco Polo notes that so far back as the 10th century it was one of the stations frequented by the Indian corsairs called B a w â r i j, belonging to Kachh and Gujarat.

(32) Returning to the mainland the narrative conducts us next to M o s k h a, a seaport trading with K a n ê, and a wintering place for vessels arriving late in the season from Malabar and the Gulf of Khambât. The distance of this place from Suagros is set down at upwards of 1,100 stadia, 600 of which represent the breadth of a bay which begins at the Cape, and is called O m a n a A l-K a m a r. The occurrence of the two names Omana and Moskha in such close connexion led D'Anville to suppose that M o s k h a is identical with M a s k a t, the capital of O m a n, the country lying at the south-east extremity of Arabia, and hence that Ras-el-Ḥad, beyond which Maskat lies, must be Cape Suagros. This supposition is, however, untenable, since the identification of Moskha with the modern A u s e r a is complete. For, in the first place, the Bay of Seger, which begins at Cape Fartak, is of exactly the same measure-

which the *Sakhalitik* frankincense is forwarded. It is regularly frequented by a number
of ships from Kanê; and such ships as come
from Limurikê and Barugaza too late in the
season put into harbour here for the winter,
where they dispose of their muslins, corn, and
oil to the king's officers, receiving in exchange
frankincense, which lies in piles throughout the

---

ment across to Cape Thurbot Ali as the Bay of
Omana, and again the distance from Cape Thurbot Ali [lat. 16° 38′ N., long. 53° 3′ E.] to Ras-al-
Sair, the Ausara of Ptolemy, corresponds almost
as exactly to the distance assigned by our author
from the same Cape to Moskha. Moreover
Pliny (XII. 35) notices that one particular kind
of incense bore the name of *Ausaritis*, and, as the
Periplûs states that Moskha was the great
emporium of the incense trade, the identification
is satisfactory.

There was another Moskha on this coast which
was also a port. It lay to the west of Suagros,
and has been identified with Keshîn [lat. 15° 21′
N. long. 51° 39′ E.]. Our author, though correct in
his description of the coast, may perhaps have erred
in his nomenclature; and this is the more likely
to have happened as it scarcely admits of doubt
that he had no personal knowledge of South
Arabia beyond Kanê and Cape Suagros.
Besides no other author speaks of an Omana
so far to westward as the position assigned to
the Bay of that name. The tract immediately
beyond Moskha or Ausera is low and fertile,

whole of S a k h a l i t i s without a guard to
protect it, as if the locality were indebted to
some divine power for its security. Indeed, it
is impossible to procure a cargo, either publicly or
by connivance, without the king's permission.
Should one take furtively on board were it but
a single grain, his vessel can by no possibility
escape from harbour.

---

and is called D ò f a r or Z h a f â r, after a famous
city now destroyed, but whose ruins are still to be
traced between Al-hâfâh and Addahariz. "This
Dhafâr," says Yule (*Marco Polo* II. p. 442 note)
"or the bold mountain above it, is supposed to
be the S e p h a r of *Genesis* X. 30." It is certain
that the Himyarites had spread their dominion as
far eastward as this place. Marco Polo thus describes Dhafâr :—" It stands upon the sea, and has
a very good haven, so that there is a great traffic
of shipping between this and India; and the merchants take hence great numbers of Arab horses
to that market, making great profits thereby. . . .
Much white incense is produced here, and I will
tell you how it grows. The trees are like small
fir-trees ; these are notched with a knife in several
places, and from these notches the incense is
exuded. Sometimes, also, it flows from the tree
without any notch, this is by reason of the great
heat of the sun there." Müller would identify
M o s k h a with Zhafâr, and accounts for the discre-
pancy of designation by supposing that our author
had confounded the name M a s k a t, which was
the great seat of the traffic in frankincense with

m

33. From the port of M o s k h a onward to
A s i k h, a distance of about 1,500 stadia, runs
a range of hills pretty close to the shore, and at
its termination there are seven islands bearing
the name of Z ê n o b i o s, beyond which again
we come to another barbarous district not
subject to any power in Arabia, but to Persis.
If when sailing by this coast you stand well out

---

the name of the greatest city in the district which
actually produced it. A similar confusion he
thinks transferred the name of Oman to the
same part of the country. The climate of the incense country is described as being extremely unhealthy, but its unhealthiness seems to have been
designedly exaggerated.

(33) Beyond M o s k h a the coast is mountainous as far as A s i k h and the islands of Zeno-
bios—a distance excessively estimated at 1,500
stadia. The mountains referred to are 5,000 feet in
height, and are those now called Subaha. A s i k h is
readily to be identified with the H â s e k of Arabian
geographers. Edrisi (I. p. 54) says: "Thence
(from Marbat) to the town of Hâsek is a four
days' journey and a two days' sail. Before H a s e k
are the two islands of K h a r t a n and M a r t a n.
Above H â s e k is a high mountain named S o u s,
which commands the sea. It is an inconsiderable
town but populous." This place is now in ruins,
but has left its name to the promontory on which
it stood [Râs Hâsek, lat. 17° 23′ N. long. 55° 20′
E. opposite the island of Hasiki]. The islands of
Z ê n o b i o s are mentioned by Ptolemy as seven in

to sea so as to keep a direct course, then at
about a distance from the island of Z ê n o b i o s
of 2,000 stadia you arrive at another island,
called that of S a r a p i s, lying off shore, say, 120
stadia. It is about 200 stadia broad and 600
long, possessing three villages inhabited by a
savage tribe of I k h t h y o p h a g o i, who speak
the Arabic language, and whose clothing con-

---

number, and are those called by Edrisi K h a r t a n
and M a r t a n, now known as the K u r i y â n
M u r i y â n islands. The inhabitants belonged to
an Arab tribe which was spread from Hasek to
Râs-el-Ḥad, and was called B e i t or Beni J e n a b i,
whence the Greek name. M. Polo in the 31st
chapter of his travels "discourseth of the two
islands called Male and Female," the position of
which he vaguely indicates by saying that "when
you leave the kingdom of K e s m a c o r a n (Mekran) which is on the mainland, you go by sea
some 500 miles towards the south, and then you
find the 2 islands Male and Female lying about
30 miles distant from one another." (See also
Marco Polo, vol. II. p. 396 note.)

Beyond A s i k h is a district inhabited by
barbarians, and subject not to Arabia but to Persis.
Then succeeds at a distance of 200 stadia beyond the
islands of Z e n o b i o s the island of S a r a p i s,
(the Ogyris of Pliny) now called Masira [lat. 20°
10′ to 20° 42′ N., long. 58° 37′ to 58° 59′ E.] opposite
that part of the coast where Oman now begins.
The *Periplûs* exaggerates both its breadth and its
distance from the continent. It was still in-

sists of a girdle made from the leaves of the
cocoa-palm. The island produces in great
plenty tortoise of excellent quality, and the
merchants of K a n ê accordingly fit out little
boats and cargo-ships to trade with it.

34. If sailing onward you wind round with
the adjacent coast to the north, then as you
approach the entrance of the Persian Gulf you

---

habited by a tribe of fish-eaters in the time of
Ebn Batuta, by whom it was visited.

On proceeding from S a r a p i s the adjacent
coast bends round, and the direction of the voyage
changes to north. The great cape which forms
the south-eastern extremity of Arabia called R â s-
e l-H a d [lat. 22° 33′ N. long. 59° 48′ E.] is here
indicated, but without being named; Ptolemy
calls it K o r o d a m o n (VI. vii. 11.)

(34) Beyond it, and near the entrance to the
Persian Gulf, occurs, according to the *Periplûs*, a
group of many islands, which lie in a range along
the coast over a space of 2,000 stadia, and are
called the islands of K a l a i o u. Here our author
is obviously in error, for there are but three groups
of islands on this coast, which are not by any
means near the entrance of the Gulf. They lie
beyond Maskat [lat. 23° 38′ N. long. 58° 36′ E.] and
extend for a considerable distance along the
Batinah coast. The central group is that of the
Deymâniyeh islands (probably the Damnia of
Pliny) which are seven in number, and lie nearly
opposite Birkeh [lat 23° 42′ N. long. 57° 55′ E.].
The error, as Müller suggests, may be accounted

fall in with a group of islands which lie in a range along the coast for 2,000 stadia, and are called the islands of K a l a i o u. The inhabitants of the adjacent coast are cruel and treacherous, and see imperfectly in the daytime.

35. ·Near the last headland of the islands of K a l a i o u is the mountain called K a l o n

---

for by supposing that the tract of country called El Baṭinah was mistaken for islands. This tract, which is very low and extremely fertile, stretches from Birkeh [lat. 23° 42′ N. long. 57° 55′ E.] onward to Jibba, where high mountains approach the very shore, and run on in an unbroken chain to the mouth of the Persian Gulf. The islands are not mentioned by any other author, for the C a l a e o u i n s u l a e of Pliny (VI. xxxii. 150) must, to avoid utter confusion, be referred to the coast of the Arabian Gulf. There is a place called E l K i l ḥ a t, the Akilla of Pliny [lat. 22° 40′ N. long. 59° 24′ E.]—but whether this is connected with the K a l a i o u islands of the *Periplûs* is uncertain [Conf. *Ind. Ant.* vol. IV. p. 48. El Kilḥât, south of Maskat and close to Ṣûr, was once a great port.]

(35) Before the mouth of the Persian Gulf is reached occurs a height called K a l o n (Fair Mount) at the last head of the islands of Papias—τῶν Παπίου νήσων. This reading has been altered by Fabricius and Schwanbeck to τῶν Καλάιου νήσων. The Fair Mount, according to Vincent, would answer sufficiently to Cape Fillam, if

(Pulcher),[30] to which succeeds, at no great distance, the month of the Persian Gulf, where there are very many pearl fisheries. On the left of the entrance, towering to a vast height, are the mountains which bear the name of A s a b o i, and directly opposite

---

that be high land, and not far from Fillam are the straits. The great cape which Arabia protrudes at these straits towards Karmania is now called Ras Mussendom. It was seen from the opposite coast by the expedition under Nearkhos, to whom it appeared to be a day's sail distant. The height on that coast is called Semiramis, and also Strongylê from its round shape. Mussendom, the 'Asabôn akron' of Ptolemy, Vincent says, "is a sort of Lizard Point to the Gulf; for all the Arabian ships take their departure from it with some ceremonies of superstition, imploring a blessing on their voyage, and setting afloat a toy like a vessel rigged and decorated, which if it is dashed to pieces by the rocks is to be accepted by the ocean as an offering for the escape of the vessel." [The straits between the island of Mussendom and the mainland are called El·Bab, and this is the origin of the name of the Papiæ islands.—Miles' *Jour. R. A. Soc.* N. S. vol. x. p. 168.]

The actual width of the straits is 40 miles. Pliny gives it at 50, and the *Periplûs* at 75. Cape Mussendom is represented in the *Periplûs* as in

---

[30] "This" (Mons Pulcher) says Major-General Miles, "is Jebel Lahrim or Shaum, the loftiest and most conspicuous peak on the whole cape (Mussendom), being nearly 7,000 feet high."—*Jour. R. As. Soc.* (N.S.) vol. X. p. 168.—Ed.

on the right you see another mountain high and
round, called the hill of Semiramis. The
strait which separates them has a width of
600 stadia, and through this opening the Persian
Gulf pours its vast expanse of waters far up
into the interior. At the very head of this gulf

Ptolemy by the Mountains of the Asabi which
are described as tremendous heights, black, grim,
and abrupt. They are named from the tribe of
Beni Asab.

We enter now the Gulf itself, and here the *Periplûs* mentions only two particulars: the famous
Pearl Fisheries which begin at the straits and
extend to Bahrein, and the situation of a regular
trading mart called Apologos, which lies at
the very head of the Gulf on the Euphrates, and in
the vicinity of Spasinou Kharax. This
place does not appear to be referred to in any
other classical work, but it is frequently
mentioned by Arabian writers under the name of
Oboleh or Obolegh. As an emporium it took
the place of Terêdôn or Diridôtis, just as
Basra (below which it was situated) under the
second Khaliphate took the place of Oboleh
itself. According to Vincent, Oboleh, or a village
that represents it, still exists between Basra and the
Euphrates. The canal also is called the canal of
Oboleh. Kharax Pasinou was situated where
the Karun (the Eulaeus of the ancients)
flows into the Pasitigris, and is represented
by the modern trading town Muhammarah.
It was founded by Alexander the Great, and after its

there is a regular mart of commerce, called the
city of A p o l o g o s, situate néar P a s i n o u-
K h a r a x and the river Euphrates.

36. If you coast along the mouth of the
gulf you are conducted by a six days' voyage to
another seat of trade belonging to Persis, called
O m a n a.[21] Barugaza maintains a regular
commercial intercourse with both these Persian

destruction, was rebuilt by Antiokhos Epiphanes,
who changed its name from Alexandreia to Antio-
kheia. It was afterwards occupied by an Arab
Chief called Pasines, or rather S p a s i n e s, who
gave it the name by which it is best known. Pliny
states that the original town was only 10 miles
from the sea, but that in his time the existing
place was so much as 120 miles from it. It was
the birth-place of two eminent geographers—
Dionysius Periegetes and Isidôros.

(36) After this cursory glance at the great
gulf, our author returns to the straits, and at once

[21] "The city of Omana is Soḥar, the ancient capital of
Omana, which name, as is well known, it then bore, and
Pliny is quite right in correcting *former writers* who had
placed it in Caramania, on which coast there is no good
evidence that there was a place of this name. Nearchus
does not mention it, and though the author of the *Periplûs
of the Erythræan Sea* does locate it in Persis, it is pretty
evident he never visited the place himself, and he must
have mistaken the information he obtained from others.
It was this city of Soḥar most probably that bore the appellation of Emporium Persarum, in which, as Philostorgius
relates, permission was given to Theophilus, the ambassador
of Constantine, to erect a Christian church." The Homna
of Pliny may be a repetition of Omana or Soḥar, which
he had already mentioned.—Miles in *Jour. R. As. Soc.*
(N. S.) vol. X. pp. 164-5.—ED.

ports, despatching thither large vessels freighted
with copper, sandalwood, beams for rafters,
horn, and logs of sasamina and ebony. Omana
imports also frankincense from Kanê, while it
exports to Arabia a particular species of vessels
called *madara*, which have their planks sewn
together. But both from A p o l o g o s and
O m a n a there are exported to Barugaza and
to Arabia great quantities of pearl, of mean
quality however compared with the Indian sort,
together with purple, cloth for the natives,
wine, dates in great quantity, and gold and
slaves.

37. After leaving the district of O m a n a

---

conducts us to the Eastern shores of the Erythraean, where occurs another emporium belonging
to Persis, at a distance from the straits of 6
courses or 3,000 stadia. This is Omana. It is
mentioned by Pliny (VI. xxxii. 149) who makes it
belong to Arabia, and accuses preceding writers
for placing it in Karmania.

The name of O m a n a has been corrupted in
the MSS. of Ptolemy into Nommana, Nombana,
K o m m a n a, Kombana, but Marcian has preserved the correct spelling. From Omana as from
Apologos great quantities of pearl of an inferior
sort were exported to Arabia and Barugaza. No
part however of the produce of India is mentioned
as among its exports, although it was the centre
of commerce between that country and Arabia.

(37) The district which succeeds Omana belongs
to the P a r s i d a i, a tribe in Gedrosia next neigh-

n

the country of the P a r s i d a i succeeds, which
belongs to another government, and the bay
which bears the name of T e r a b d o i, from the
midst of which a cape projects. Here also is
a river large enough to permit the entrance of
ships, with a small mart at its mouth called
O r a i a. Behind it in the interior, at the
distance of a seven days' journey from the coast,
is the city where the king resides, called Rham-
bakia. This district, in addition to corn, produces wine, rice, and dates, though in the tract
near the sea, only the fragrant gum called
bdellium.

---

bours to the A r b i t a e on the East. They are
mentioned by Ptolemy (VI. xx., p. 439) and by
Arrian (*Indika* xxvi.) who calls them P a s i-
r e e s, and notes that they had a small town
called P a s i r a, distant about 60 stadia from the
sea, and a harbour with good anchorage called
B a g i s a r a. The Promontory of the *Periplús* is
also noted and described as projecting far into the
sea, and being high and precipitous. It is the Cape
now called A r a b a h or U r m a r a h. The Bay
into which it projects is called T e r a b d ô n, a
name which is found only in our author.
Vincent erroneously identifies this with the P a r a-
g ô n of Ptolemy. It is no doubt the Bay which
extends from Cape Guadel to Cape Monze. The
river which enters this Bay, at the mouth of which
stood the small mart called O r a i a, was probably
that which is now called the Akbor. The royal city

38. After this region, where the coast is already deeply indented by gulfs caused by the land advancing with a vast curve from the east, succeeds the seaboard of Skythia, a region which extends to northward. It is very low and flat, and contains the mouths of the S i n t h o s (Indus), the largest of all the rivers which fall into the Erythræan Sea, and which, indeed, pours into it such a vast body of water that while you are yet far off from the land at its mouth you find the sea turned of a white colour by its waters.

The sign by which voyagers before sighting

---

which lay inland from the sea a seven days' journey was perhaps, as Mannert has conjectured, R a m b a k i a, mentioned by Arrian (*Anab.* vi. 21) as the capital of the O r e i t a i or H o r i t a i.

(38) We now approach the mouths of the Indus which our author calls the S i n t h o s, transliterating the native name of it—S i n d h u. In his time the wide tract which was watered by this river in the lower part of its course was called I n d o s k y t h i a. It derived its name from the Skythian tribes (the Ś â k a of Sansk.) who after the overthrow of the Graeco-Baktrian empire gradually passed southward to the coast, where they established themselves about the year 120 B. C., occupying all the region between the Indus and the Narmadâ. They are called by Dionysios Periegetes N o t i o i S k y t h a i, the Southern Skythians. Our author mentions two cities which

land know that it is near is their meeting with
serpents floating on the water; but higher up
and on the coasts of Persia the first sign of land
is seeing them of a different kind, called *graai*.
[Sansk. *graha*—an alligator.] The river has seven
mouths, all shallow, marshy and unfit for navigation except only the middle stream, on which
is B a r b a r i k o n, a trading seaport. Before
this town lies a small islet, and behind it in the
interior is M i n n a g a r, the metropolis of
Skythia, which is governed, however, by Parthian
princes, who are perpetually at strife among
themselves, expelling each the other.

39. Ships accordingly anchor near B a r b a-
r i k ê, but all their cargoes are conveyed by the
river up to the king, who resides in the metropolis.

The articles imported into this emporium are—
'Ιματισμὸς 'απλοῦς ἱκανὸς—Clothing, plain and
in considerable quantity.

---

belonged to them—B a r b a r i k o n and M i n n a-
g a r; the former of which was an emporium
situated near the sea on the middle and only navigable branch of the Indus. Ptolemy has a B a r -
b a r e i in the Delta, but the position he assigns
to it, does not correspond with that of B a r b a r i -
k o n. M i n n a g a r was the Skythian metropolis.
It lay inland, on or near the banks of the Indus.

(39) Ships did not go up to it but remained at
B a r b a r i k o n, their cargoes being conveyed up
the river in small boats. In Ptolemy (VII. i. 61)

Ἱματισμὸς νόθος οὐ πολὺς—Clothing, mixed, not much.

Πολύμιτα—Flowered cottons.

Χρυσόλιθον—Yellow-stone, topazes.

Κοράλλιον—Coral.

Στύραξ—Storax.

Λίβανος—Frankincense (*Lóbán*).

Ὑαλά σκεύη—Glass vessels. *Y Se infra 123*

Αργυρώματα—Silver plate.

Χρῆμα—Specie.

Οἶνος οὐ πολύς—Wine, but not much.

The exports are :—

Κόστος—Costus, a spice.

Βδέλλα—Bdellium, a gum.

Λύκιον—A yellow dye (*Ruzót*).

Νάρδος—Spikenard.

Λίθος καλλαϊνος—Emeralds or green-stones.

Σάπφειρος—Sapphires.

Σηρικὰ δέρματα—Furs from China.

Ὀθόνιον—Cottons.

Νῆμα Σηρικὸν—Silk thread.

Ἰνδικὸν μέλαν—Indigo.

---

the form of the name is B i n a g a r a, which is less correct since the word is composed of *Min*, the Indian name for the Skythians, and *nagar*, a city. Ritter considers that T h a ṭ h a is its modern representative, since it is called S a m i n a g a r by the Jâḍejâ Rajputs who, though settled in Kachh, derive their origin from that city. To this view it is objected that Ṭhaṭha is not near the position which Ptolemy assigns to his B i n a g a r a. Mannert places it at B a k k a r, D'Anville at M a n s u r a, and Vincent at M e n h a b e r y mentioned

Ships destined for this port put out to sea
when the Indian monsoon prevails—that is,
about the month of July or Epiphi. The
voyage at this season is attended with danger,
but being shorter is more expeditious.

---

by Edrisi (I. p. 164) as distant two stations or 60
miles from D a b i l, which again was three stations
or 90 miles from the mouth of the Indus, that is
it lay at the head of the Delta. Our author informs
us that in his time M i n a g a r was ruled by
Parthian princes. The Parthians (the Parada of
Sanskrit writers) must therefore have subverted
a Skythian dynasty which must have been that
which (as Benfey has shown) was founded by
Y e n k a o t s c h i n between the years 30 and 20
B.C., or about 30 years only after the famous Indian
Æra called *Śákábda* (the year of the Śáka) being
that in which Vikramâditya expelled the Skythians
from Indian soil. The statement of the *Periplûs*
that Parthian rulers succeeded the Skythian is
confirmed by Parthian coins found everywhere
in this part of the country. These sovereigns
must have been of consequence, or the trade
of their country very lucrative to the merchant
as appears by the presents necessary to ensure his
protection—plate, musical instruments, handsome
girls for the Harem, the best wine, plain cloth of
high price, and the finest perfumes. The profits
of the trade must therefore have been great, but if
Pliny's account be true, that every pound laid out
in India produced a hundred at Rome, greater
exactions than these might easily have been supported.

40. After the river S i n t h o s is passed we
reach another gulf, which cannot be easily seen.
It has two divisions,—the Great and the Little
by name,—both shoal with violent and continuous
eddies extending far out from the shore, so that
before ever land is in sight ships are often
grounded on the shoals, or being caught within
the eddies are lost. Over this gulf hangs a
promontory which, curving from E i r i n o n first
to the east, then to the south, and finally to the
west, encompasses the gulf called B a r a k ê,
in the bosom of which lie seven islands.
Should a vessel approach the entrance of
this gulf, the only chance of escape for those on
board is at once to alter their course and stand
out to sea, for it is all over with them if they
are once fairly within the womb of B a r a k ê,

---

(40) The first place mentioned after the Indus
is the Gulf of E i r i n o n, a name of which traces
remain in the modern appellation the R a ṇ of
Kachh. This is no longer covered with water
except during the monsoon, when it is flooded by
sea water or by rains and inundated rivers. At
other seasons it is not even a marsh, for its bed is
hard, dry and sandy; a mere saline waste almost
entirely devoid of herbage, and frequented but by
one quadruped—the wild ass. Burnes conjectured
that its desiccation resulted from an upheaval
of the earth caused by one of those earthquakes
which are so common in that part of India.
The R a ṇ is connected with the Gulf of Kachh,

which surges with vast and mighty billows,
and where the sea, tossing in violent commotion,
forms eddies and impetuous whirlpools in every
direction. The bottom varies, presenting in
places sudden shoals, in others being scabrous
with jagged rocks, so that when an anchor
grounds its cable is either at once cut through,
or soon broken by friction at the bottom. The
sign by which voyagers know they are approaching this bay is their seeing serpents floating
about on the water, of extraordinary size and of
a black colour, for those met with lower down
and in the neighbourhood of Barugaza are of
less size, and in colour green and golden.

41. To the gulf of B a r a k ê succeeds that

---

which our author calls the Gulf of B a r a k ê.
His account of it is far from clear. Perhaps, as
Müller suggests, he comprehended under E i r i-
n o n the interior portion of the Gulf of Kachh,
limiting the Gulf of B a r a k ê to the exterior portion or entrance to it. This gulf is called that of
Kanthi by Ptolemy, who mentions B a r a k ê only
as an island, [and the south coast of Kachh is
still known by the name of Kantha]. The islands
of the *Periplûs* extend westward from the neighbourhood of N a v a n a g a r to the very entrance
of the Gulf.

(41) To B a r a k ê succeeds the Gulf of B a r u-
g a z a (Gulf of K h a m b h â t) and the sea-board
of the region called A r i a k ê. The reading of the
MS. here ἡ πρὸς Ἀραβικῆς χώρας is considered corrupt. Müller substitutes ἡ ἤπειρος τῆς Ἀριακῆς

of B a r u g a z a and the mainland of A r i a k ê,
a district which forms the frontier of the kingdom of M o m b a r o s and of all India. The
interior part of it which borders on S k y t h i a
is called A b ê r i a, and its sea-board S u r a s-
t r ê n ê. It is a region which produces abundantly corn and rice and the oil of sesamum,
butter, muslins and the coarser fabrics which are

χώρας, though Mannert and others prefer Λαρικῆς
χώρας, relying on Ptolemy, who places A r i a k ê to
the south of L a r i k ê, and says that L a r i k ê
comprehends the peninsula (of Gujarât) Barugaza·
and the parts adjacent. As A r i a k ê was however previously mentioned in the *Periplûs* (sec.
14) in connexion with Barugaza, and is afterwards
mentioned (sec. 54) as trading with Muziris, it
must no doubt have been mentioned by the author
in its proper place, which is here. [Bhagvanlâl
Indraji Pandit has shewn reasons however for
correcting the readings into Αβαρατικη, the Prakrit
form of A p a r â n t i k â, an old name of the western
sea board of India.—*Ind. Ant.* vol. VII., pp. 259,
263.] Regarding the name L a r i k ê, Yule has
the following note (*Travels of M. Polo* vol. II.,
p. 353):—" L â r-D e ś a, the country of Lar," properly Lât-deśa, was an early name for the
territory of Gujrat and the northern Konkan,
embracing Saimur (the modern Chaul as I believe)
Thana, and Bharoch. It appears in Ptolemy in
the form L a r i k ê. The sea to the west of that coast
was in the early Muhammadan times called the sea
of Lâr, and the language spoken on its shores is

o

manufactured from Indian cotton. It has also numerous herds of cattle. The natives are men of large stature and coloured black. The metropolis of the district is M i n n a g a r, from which

---

called by M a s'u d i, L â r i. Abulfeda's authority, Ibn Said, speaks of Lâr and Gujarât as identical."

A r i a k ê (Aparântikâ), our author informs us, was the beginning or frontier of India. That part of the interior of Ariakê which bordered on Skythia was called A b e r i a or Abiria (in the MS. erroneously Ibêria). The corresponding Indian word is A b h î r a, which designated the district near the mouths of the river. Having been even in very early times a great seat of commerce, some (as Lassen) have been led to think from a certain similarity of the names that this was the O p h i r of scripture, a view opposed by Ritter. Abiria is mentioned by Ptolemy, who took it to be not a part of India but of Indoskythia. The sea-board of Ariakê was called S u r a s t r ê n ê, and is mentioned by Ptolemy, who says (VII. i. 55) it was the region about the mouths of the Indus and the Gulf of Kanthi. It answers to the Sanskrit S u r â s h ṭ r a. Its capital was M i n n a g a r,—a city which, as its name shows, had once belonged to the Min or Skythians. It was different of course from the Minnagar already mentioned as the capital of Indo-Skythia. It was situated to the south of O z ê n ê (Ujjayinî, or Ujjain), and on the road which led from that city to the River Narmadâ, probably near where Indôr now stands. It must have been the capital only for a short time, as Ptolemy informs us (II. i. 63) that O z ê n ê was in his time the

cotton cloth is exported in great quantity to
B a r u g a z a. In this part of the country there
are preserved even to this very day memorials
of the expedition of Alexander, old temples,
foundations of camps, and large wells. The
extent of this coast, reckoned from B a r b a-
r i k o n to the promontory called P a p i k ê, near
A s t a k a p r a, which is opposite B a r u g a z a,
is 3,000 stadia.

---

capital of T i a s h a n e s [probably the Chashṭana
of Coins and the Cave Temple inscriptions]. From
both places a great variety of merchandise was
sent down the Narmadâ to Barugaza.

The next place our author mentions is a promontory called P a p i k ê projecting into the Gulf
of Khambât from that part of the peninsula of
Gujarât which lies opposite to the Barugaza coast.
Its distance from Barbarikon on the middle mouth
of the Indus is correctly given at 3,000 stadia.
This promontory is said to be near A s t a k a p r a,
a place which is mentioned also by Ptolemy, and
which (*Ind. Ant.* vol. V. p. 314) has been identified by
Colonel Yule with H a s t a k a v a p r a (now H â-
t h a b near Bhaunagar), a name which occurs in
a copper-plate grant of Dhruvasena I of Valabhi.
With regard to the Greek form of this name
Dr. Bühler thinks it is not derived immediately
from the Sanskrit, but from an intermediate old
Prakrit word Hastakampra, which had been
formed by the contraction of the syllables *ava*
to *â*, and the insertion of a nasal, according to
the habits of the Gujarâtis. The loss of the

42. After Papikê there is another gulf,
exposed to the violence of the waves and
running up to the north. Near its mouth is an
island called Baiônês, and at its very head it
receives a vast river called the Maîs. Those
bound for Barugaza sail up this gulf (which
has a breadth of about 300 stadia), leaving the
island on the left till it is scarcely visible in the
horizon, when they shape their course east for
the mouth of the river that leads to Barugaza.
This is called the Namnadios.

---

initial, he adds, may be explained by the difficulty
which Gujarâtîs have now and probably had 1,600
years ago in pronouncing the *spirans* in its proper
place. The modern name Hâthab or Hâthap may
be a corruption of the shorter Sanskrit form
Hastavapra.

(42) Beyond Papikê, we are next informed,
there is another gulf running northward into the
interior of the country. This is not really another
Gulf but only the northern portion of the Gulf
of Khambât, which the *Periplûs* calls the Gulf of
Barugaza. It receives a great river, the Maîs,
which is easily identified with the Mahi, and
contains an island called Baiônês [the modern
Peram], which you leave on the left hand as you
cross over from Astakapra to Barugaza.

We are now conducted to Barugaza, the
greatest seat of commerce in Western India,
situated on a river called in the MS. of the *Periplûs*
the Lamnaios, which is no doubt an erroneous
reading for Namados, or Namnados or Namna-

43. The passage into the gulf of B a r u-
g a z a is narrow and difficult of access to those
approaching it from the sea, for they are carried
either to the right or to the left, the left being
the better passage of the two. On the right,
at the very entrance of the gulf, lies a narrow
stripe of shoal, rough and beset with rocks. It
is called H ê r ô n ê, and lies opposite the village
of K a m m ô n i. On the left side right against
this is the promontory of P a p i k ê, which lies
in front of A s t a k a p r a, where it is difficult to
anchor, from the strength of the current and
because the cables are cut through by the sharp
rocks at the bottom. But even if the passage
into the gulf is secured the mouth of the
Barugaza river is not easy to hit, since the coast
is low and there are no certain marks to be seen
until you are close upon them. Neither, if it is
discovered, is it easy to enter, from the presence
of shoals at the mouth of the river.

---

dios. This river is the N a r m a d â. It is called
by Ptolemy the Namadês.

(43) B a r u g a z a (Bharoch) which was 30
miles distant from its mouth, was both difficult and
dangerous of access ; for the entrance to the Gulf
itself was, on the right, beset with a perilous stripe
(*tainia*) of rocky shoal called H e r ô n ê, and on the
left, (which was the safer course,) the violent
currents which swept round the promontory of
Papikê rendered it unsafe to approach the shore or
to cast anchor. The shoal of Herônê was opposite

44. For this reason native fishermen appointed by Government are stationed with well-manned long boats called *trappaga* and *kotumba* at the entrance of the river, whence they go out as far as S u r a s t r ê n ê to meet ships, and pilot them up to Barugaza. At the head of the gulf the pilot, immediately on taking charge of a ship, with the help of his own boat's crew, shifts her head to keep her clear of the shoals, and tows her from one fixed station to another, moving with the beginning of the tide, and dropping anchor at certain roadsteads and basins when it ebbs. These basins occur at points where the river is deeper than usual, all the way up to B a r u g a z a, which is 300 stadia distant from the mouth of the river if you sail up the stream to reach it.

45. India has everywhere a great abundance of rivers, and her seas ebb and flow with tides of extraordinary strength, which increase with

---

a village on the mainland called K a m m ô n i, the Kamanê of Ptolemy (VII. i.), who however places it to the north of the river's mouth. Again, it was not only difficult to hit the mouth of the river, but its navigation was endangered by sandbanks and the violence of the tides, especially the high tide called the ' Bore,' of which our author gives a description so particular and so vivid as suffices to show that he was describing what he had seen with his own eyes, and seen moreover for the first time. With regard to the name

the moon, both when new and when full, and for three days after each, but fall off in the intermediate space. About B a r u g a z a they are more violent than elsewhere; so that all of a sudden you see the depths laid bare, and portions of the land turned into sea, and the sea, where ships were sailing but just before, turned without warning into dry land. The rivers, again, on the access of flood tide rushing into their channels with the whole body of the sea, are driven upwards against their natural course for a great number of miles with a force that is irresistible.

46. This is the reason why ships frequenting this emporium are exposed, both in coming and going, to great risk, if handled by those who are unacquainted with the navigation of the gulf or visit it for the first time, since the impetuosity of the tide when it becomes full, having nothing to stem or slacken it, is such that

---

B a r u g a z a the following passage, which I quote from Dr. Wilson's *Indian Castes* (vol. II. p. 113) will elucidate its etymology :—" The B h â r g a v a s derive their designation from B h a r g a v a, the adjective form of B h ṛ i g u, the name of one of the ancient Ṛishis. Their chief habitat is the district of Bharoch, which must have got its name from a colony of the school of Bhṛigu having been early established in this Kshêtra, probably granted to them by some conqueror of the district. In the name B a r u g a z a given to it by Ptolemy, we have

anchors cannot hold against it. Large vessels, moreover, if caught in it are driven athwart from their course by the rapidity of the current till they are stranded on shoals and wrecked, while the smaller craft are capsized, and many that have taken refuge in the side channels, being left dry by the receding tide, turn over on one side, and, if not set erect on props, are filled upon the return of the tide with the very first head of the flood, and sunk. But at new moons, especially when they occur in conjunction with a night tide, the flood sets in with such extraordinary violence that on its beginning to advance, even though the sea be calm, its roar is heard by those living near the river's mouth, sounding like the tumult of battle heard far off, and soon after the sea with its hissing waves bursts over the bare shoals.

See JRAS. 1913 127 - 30

✕ 47. Inland from B a r u g a z a the country is inhabited by numerous races—the A r a t r i o i,

---

a Greek corruption of Bhṛigukshêtra (the territory of Bhṛigu) or Bhṛigukachha (the tongueland of Bhṛigu)." Speaking of the Bhârgavas Dr. Drummond, in his *Grammatical Illustrations*, says:— "These Brâhmans are indeed poor and ignorant. Many of them, and other illiterate Gujarâtîs, would, in attempting to articulate Bhṛigushêtra, lose the half in coalesence, and call it Bargacha, whence the Greeks, having no *Ch*, wrote it Barugaza."

(47) The account of the 'bore' is followed by an

and the A̱rakhôsioi, and the Gandaraioi,
and the people of Proklaïs, in which is
Boukephalos Alexandreia. Beyond
these are the Baktrianoi, a most warlike
race, governed by their own independent sovereign. It was from these parts Alexander issued
to invade India when he marched as far as the
Ganges, without, however, attacking Limurikê
and the southern parts of the country. Hence
up to the present day old *drachmai* bearing the

---

enumeration of the countries around and beyond
Barugaza with which it had commercial relations.
Inland are the Aratrioi, Arakhosioi,
Gandarioi and the people of Proklais, a
province wherein is Boukephalos Alexandreia,
beyond which is the Baktrian nation. It has
been thought by some that by the Aratrioi are
meant the Arii, by others that they were the
A̱rā̱strā̱s of Sanskrit called Aratti in the
Prakrit, so that the Aratrioi of the *Periplûs*
hold an intermediate place between the Sanskrit and
Prakrit form of the name. Müller however says
" if you want a people known to the Greeks and
Romans as familiarly as the well-known names
of the Arakhosii, Gandarii, Peukelitae, you may
conjecture that the proper reading is ΔΡΑΙΤΩΝ instead of ΑΡΑΤΡΙΩΝ. It is an error of course on the
part of our author when he places Boukephalos
(a city built by Alexander on the banks of the
Hydaspês, where he defeated Pôros), in the neighbourhood of Proklais, that is Pekhely in the neighbourhood of Peshawar. He makes a still more

p

Greek inscriptions of A p o l l o d o t o s and
M e n a n d e r are current in Barugaza.

48. In the same region eastward is a city
called O z ê n ê, formerly the capital wherein
the king resided. From it there is brought
down to Barugaza every commodity for the
supply of the country and for export to our
own markets—onyx-stones, porcelain, fine muslins, mallow-coloured muslins, and no small
quantity of ordinary cottons. At the same time
there is brought down to it from the upper
country by way of P r o k l a ï s, for transmis-
sion to the coast, Kattybourine, Patropapigic,
and Kabalitic spikenard, and another kind
which reaches it by way of the adjacent province
of Skythia; also kostus and bdellium.

49. The imports of B a r u g a z a are—

Οἶνος προηγουμένως Ἰταλικὸς—Wine, principally
Italian.

Καὶ Λαοδικηνὸς καὶ Ἀραβικὸς—Laodikean wine
and Arabian.

Χαλκὸς καὶ κασσίτερος καὶ μόλυβδος—Brass or
Copper and Tin and Lead.

Κοράλλιον καὶ χρυσόλιθον—Coral and Gold-stone
or Yellow-stone.

---

surprising error when he states that Alexander
penetrated to the Ganges.

(48) The next place mentioned in the enumeration is O z ê n ê (Ujjain), which, receiving
nard through Proklais from the distant regions
where it was produced, passed it on to the
coast for export to the Western World. This

'Ιματισμὸς ἀπλοῦς καὶ νόθος πανταῖος—Cloth, plain and mixed, of all sorts.

Πολύμιται ζῶναι πηχναῖαι—Variegated sashes half a yard wide.

Στύραξ—Storax.

Μελίλωτον—Sweet clover, melilot.

Ὕαλος ἀργή—White glass.

Σανδαράκη—Gum Sandarach.

Στίμμι—(Stibium) Tincture for the eyes,—*Sûrmâ*.

Δηνάριον χρυσοῦ καὶ ἀργυροῦν—Gold and Silver specie, yielding a profit when exchanged for native money.

Μύρον οὐ βαρύτιμον οὐδὲ πολὺ—Perfumes or unguents, neither costly nor in great quantity.

In those times, moreover, there were imported, *as presents* to the king, costly silver vases, instruments of music, handsome young women for concubinage, superior wine, apparel, plain but costly, and the choicest unguents. The exports from this part of the country are—

Νάρδος, κόστος, βδέλλα, ἐλέφας—Spikenard, costus, bdellium, ivory.

'Ονυχίνη λιθία καὶ μουρρίνη—Onyx-stones and porcelain.

Λύκιον—*Ruzot*, Box-thorn.

---

aromatic was a product of three districts, whence its varieties were called respectively the *Kattybourine*, the *Patropapigic* and the *Kabolitic*. What places were indicated by the first two names cannot be ascertained, but the last points undoubtedly to the region round Kâbul, since its inhabitants are called by Ptolemy K a b o l i t a i, and Edrisi uses the term *Myrobalanos Kabolinos*

'Οθόνιον παντοῖον—Cottons of all sorts.

Σηρικὸν—Silk.

Μολόχινον—Mallow-coloured cottons.

Νῆμα—*Silk* thread.

Πέπερι μακρὸν—Long pepper and other articles supplied from the neighbouring ports.

The proper season to set sail for Barugaza from Egypt is the month of July, or Epiphi.

50. From B a r u g a z a the coast immediately adjoining stretches from the north directly to the south, and the country is therefore called D a k h i n a b a d ê s, because Dakhan in the language of the natives signifies *south*. Of this country that part which lies inland towards the east comprises a great space of desert country, and large mountains abounding with all kinds of wild animals, leopards, tigers, elephants, huge snakes, hyenas, and baboons of many different sorts, and is inhabited right across to the Ganges by many and extremely populous nations.

---

for the 'myrobolans of Kâbul.' Nard, as Edrisi also observes, has its proper soil in Thibet.

(50) B a r u g a z a had at the same time commercial relations with the Dekhan also. This part of India our author calls D a k h i n a b a d ê s, transliterating the word D a k s h i n â p a t h a—(the Dakshinâ, or the South Country). "Here," says Vincent, "the author of the *Periplûs* gives the true direction of this western coast of the Peninsula, and states in direct terms its tendency to the South, while Ptolemy stretches out the whole angle to a straight line, and places the Gulf of

51.   Among the marts in this South Country
there are two of more particular importance—
P a i t h a n a, which lies south from Barugaza,
a distance of twenty days, and T a g a r a, ten
days east of Paithana, the greatest city in the
country.   Their commodities are carried down
on wagons to Barugaza along roads of extreme
difficulty,—that is, from P a i t h a n a a great

Cambay almost in the same latitude as Cape
Comorin."

(51)   In the interior of the Dekhan, the *Periplûs*
places two great seats of commerce, P a i t h a n a,
20 days' journey to the south of Barugaza, and
T a g a r a, 10 days' journey eastward from Paithana.   Paithana, which appears in Ptolemy as
Baithana, may be identified with P a i t h a n a.
T a g a r a is more puzzling.   Wilford, Vincent,
Mannert, Ritter and others identify it with D ê v a-
g i r i or Deogarh, near Elurâ, about 8 miles from
Aurangâbâd.   The name of a place called Tagara-
pura occurs in a copper grant of land which was
found in the island of Salsette.   There is however
nothing to show that this was a name of Dêvagiri.
Besides, if Paithana be correctly identified, Tagara
cannot be Dêvagiri unless the distances and directions are very erroneously given in the *Periplûs*.
This is not improbable, and Tagara may therefore
be J u n n a r (*i.e.* Jûna-nagar = *the old city*), which
from its position must always have been an emporium, and its Buddha caves belong to about
B. C. 100 to A.D. 150 (see *Archæolog. Surv. of West.
India*, vol. III., and Elphinstone's *History of
India*, p. 223).

quantity of onyx-stone, and *from T a g a r a
ordinary cottons in abundance, many sorts of
muslins, mallow-coloured cottons, and other
articles of local production brought into it from
the parts along the coast. The length of the
entire voyage as far as L i m u r i k ê is 700
stadia, and to reach A i g i a l o s you must sail
very many stadia further.

Our author introduces us next to another division of India, that called L i m u r i k ê, which
begins, as he informs us, at a distance of 7,000 stadia
(or nearly 900 miles) beyond Barugaza. This
estimate is wide of the mark, being in fact about
the distance between Barugaza and the southern
or remote extremity of Limurikê. In the Indian
segment of the Roman maps called from their dis-
coverer, the *Peutinger Tables*, the portion of India
to which this name is applied is called D a m i-
r i k ê. We can scarcely err, says Dr. Caldwell
(*Dravid. Gram.* Intr. page 14), in identifying this
name with the Tamil country. If so, the earliest
appearance of the name Tamil in any foreign
documents will be found also to be most perfectly
in accordance with the native Tamil mode of
spelling the name. D a m i r i k e evidently means
Damir-ike . . . In another place in the same map
a district is called S c y t i a D y m i r i c e; and it
appears to have been this word which by a mistake of Δ for Λ Ptolemy wrote Λυμιρικὴ. The D
retains its place however in the Cosmography of
the anonymous geographer of Ravenna, who re-
peatedly mentions D i m i r i c a as one of the three
divisions of India and the one furthest to the East.

52. The local marts which occur in order
along the coast after B a r u g a z a are A k a-
b a r o u, S o u p p a r a, K a l l i e n a, a city which
was raised to the rank of a regular mart in the
times of the elder S a r a g a n e s, but after

He shows also that the Tamiḷ country must
have been meant by the name by mentioning
M o d u r a as one of the cities it contained.

(52) Reverting to B a r u g a z a our author next
enumerates the less important emporia having
merely a local trade which intervenes between it
and D i m u r i k ê. These are first A k a b a r o u,
S o u p p a r a, and K a l l i e n a—followed by
S e m u l l a, M a n d a g o r a, P a l a i p a t m a i,
M e l i g e i z a r a, B u z a n t i o n, T o p e r o n, and
T u r a n o s b o a s,—beyond which occurs a succession of islands, some of which give shelter to
pirates, and of which the last is called L e u k ê or
White Island. The actual distance from Barugaza
to Naoura, the first port of Dimurikê, is 4,500
stadia.

To take these emporia in detail. A k a b a r o u
cannot be identified. The reading is probably corrupt. Between the mouths of the Namados and
those of the Goaris, Ptolemy interposes Nousaripa,
Poulipoula, Ariakê Sadinôn, and Soupara. N a u-
s a r i p a is N a u s a r i, about 18 miles to the
south of Surat, and S o u p a r a is S û p â r â near
Vasâï. Benfey, who takes it to be the name of a
region and not of a city, regards it as the O p h i r
of the Bible—called in the Septuagint Σωφηρά.
S ô p h i r, it may be added, is the Coptic name for
India. K a l l i e n a is now K a l y â ṇ a near

Sandanes became its master its trade was
put under the severest restrictions; for if Greek
vessels, even by accident, enter its ports, a guard
is put on board and they are taken to Barugaza.

53.   After Kalliena other local marts oc-

Bombay [which must have been an important
place at an early date. It is named in the
Kaṇhêri Bauddha Cave Inscriptions].   It is
mentioned by Kosmas (p. 337), who states that
it produced copper and sesamum and other
kinds of logs, and cloth for wearing apparel.
The name Sandanes, that of the Prince who
sent Greek ships which happened to put into its
port under guard to Barugaza, is thought by
Benfey to be a territorial title which indicated
that he ruled over Ariakê of the Sandineis.
[But the elder " Saraganes" probably indicates
one of the great Sâtakarṇi or Â ndhrabhṛitya
dynasty.] Ptolemy does not mention Kalliena,
though he supplies the name of a place omitted
in the Periplús, namely Dounga (VII. i. 6)
near the mouth of the river Bênda.

(53) Semulla (in Ptolemy Timoula and
Simulla) is identified by Yule with Chênval
or Chaul, a seaport 23 miles south of Bombay;
[but Bhagvanlâl Indraji suggests Chimûla in
Trombay island at the head of the Bombay
harbour; and this is curiously supported by one
of the Kaṇhêri inscriptions in which Chomûla
is mentioned, apparently as a large city, like
Supârâ and Kalyâna, in the neighbourhood].
After Simulla Ptolemy mentions Hippo-
koura [possibly, as suggested by the same,

cur—Sêmulla, Mandagora, Palaipat-
mai, Melizeigara, Buzantion, Toparon,
and Turannosboas. You come next to the
islands called Sêsekreienai and the island

---

a partial translation of Ghoḍabandar on
the Choḍa nadi in the Ṭhaṇa strait] and Balti-
p̣atna as places still in Ariakê, but Mandagara Buzanteion, Khersonêsos, Ar-
magara, the mouths of the river Nanagouna,
and an emporium called Nitra, as belonging to
the Pirate Coast which extended to Dimurikê, of
which Tundis, he says, is the first city. Ptolemy
therefore agrees with our author in assigning the
Pirate Coast to the tract of country between
Bombay and Goa. This coast continued to be
infested with pirates till so late a period as the
year 1765, when they were finally exterminated by
the British arms. Mandagara and Palaipat-
ma may have corresponded pretty nearly in situation with the towns of Râjapur and Bankut. Yule
places them respectively at Bankut and Debal.
Melizeigara (Miliẑêguris or Miliẑigêris of
Ptolemy, VII. i. 95), Vincent identifies with Jaygaḍh
or Sidê Jaygaḍh. The same place appears in Pliny
as Sigerus (VI. xxvi. 100). Buzantium may be
referred to about Vijayadrug or Esvantgadh, Toparon may be a corrupt reading for Togaron,
and may perhaps therefore be Devagaḍh which
lies a little beyond Vijayadrug. Turannosboas
is not mentioned elsewhere, but it may have been,
as Yule suggests, the Bandâ or Tirakal river.
Müller placed it at Acharê. The first island on
this part of the coast is Sindhudrug near Mâlwan,

q

of the A i g i d i o i and that of the K a i n e i t a i,
near what is called the K h e r s o n ê s o s, places
in which are pirates, and after this the island
L e u k ê (or 'the White'). Then follow N a o u r a

to which succeeds a group called the Burnt Islands,
among which the Vingorla rocks are conspicuous.
These are no doubt the H e p t a n ê s i a of
Ptolemy (VII. i. 95), and probably the S ê s i -
k r i e n a i of the *Periplûs*. The island Aigidion
called that of the Aigidii may be placed at Goa,
[but Yule suggests Angediva south of Sadaśiva-
gaḍh, in lat. 14° 45′ N., which is better]. Kaineiton
may be the island of St. George.

We come next to N a o u r a in Dimurikê. This
is now H o n â v a r, written otherwise Onore,
situated on the estuary of a broad river, the
Ś a r â v a t î, on which are the falls of Gêrsappa,
one of the most magnificent and stupendous
cataracts in the world. If the N i t r a of Ptolemy
(VII. i. 7) and the N i t r i a of Pliny be the same as
N a o u r a, then these authors extend the pirate
coast a little further south than the *Periplûs* does.
But if they do not, and therefore agree in their
views as to where Dimurikê begins, the N i t r a
may be placed, Müller thinks, at Mirjan or Komta,
which is not far north from Honavar. [Yule
places it at Mangalur.] Müller regards the first
supposition however as the more probable, and
quotes at length a passage from Pliny (VI. xxvi.
104) referring thereto, which must have been ex-
cerpted from some *Periplûs* like our author's, but
not from it as some have thought. " To those
bound for India it is most convenient to depart

and Tundis, the first marts of Limuriké,
and after these Mouziris and Nelkunda,
the seats of Government.

54. To the kingdom under the sway of

from Okelis. They sail thence with the wind
Hipalus in 40 days to the first emporium of India,
Muziris, which is not a desirable place to arrive
at on account of pirates infesting the neighbourhood, who hold a place called Nitrias, while it is
not well supplied with merchandize. Besides,
the station for ships is at a great distance from
the shore, and cargoes have both to be landed and
to be shipped by means of little boats. There
reigned there when I wrote this Caelobo-
thras. Another port belonging to the nation
is more convenient, Neacyndon, which is
called Becare (*sic. codd.*, Barace, Harduin and
Sillig). There reigned Pandion in an inland
town far distant from the emporium called Mo-
dura. The region, however, from which they
convey pepper to Becare in boats formed from
single logs is Cottonara."

(54) With regard to the names in this extract
which occur also in the *Periplûs* the following
passages quoted from Dr. Caldwell's *Dravidian
Grammar* will throw much light. He says (Introd.
p. 97):—"Muziris appears to be the Muyiri
of Muyiri-kotta. Tyndis is Tuṇḍi, and the
Kynda, of Nelkynda, or as Ptolemy has it, Mel-
kynda, *i. e.* probably Western kingdom, seems to
be Kannettri, the southern boundary of Kêrala
proper. One MS. of Pliny writes the second part
of this word not *Cyndon* but *Canidon.* The first

Kêprobotras[20] Tundis is subject, a village of great note situate near the sea. Mouziris, which pertains to the same realm, is a city at the height of prosperity, frequented as it

of these places was identified by Dr. Gundert, for the remaining two we are indebted to Dr. Burnell.

"Cottonara, Pliny; Kottonarike, *Periplûs*, the district where the best pepper was produced. It is singular that this district was not mentioned by Ptolemy. Cottonara was evidently the name of the district. κοττοναρικον the name of the pepper for which the district was famous. Dr. Buchanan identifies Cottonara with Kaḍatta-naḍu, the name of a district in the Calicut country celebrated for its pepper. Dr. Burnell identifies it with Koḷatta-nâḍu, the district about Telli-cherry which he says is the pepper district. *Kaḍatta* in Malayâlam means 'transport, convey-ance,' *Nâḍû*, Tam.—Mal., means a district."

"The prince called Kêrobothros by Ptolemy (VII. i. 86) is called Kêprobotros by the author of the *Periplûs*. The insertion of π is clearly an error, but more likely to be the error of a copyist than that of the author, who himself had visited the territories of the prince in question. He is called Caëlobothras in Pliny's text, but one of the MSS. gives it more correctly as Celobotras. The name in Sanskrit, and in full is 'Keralaputra,' but both *kêra* and *kêla* are Dravidian abbreviations of *kêralâ*. They are Malayâlam however, not Tamil abbrevia-tions, and the district over which Keralaputra ruled is that in which the Malayâlam language is now

[20] *Ind. Ant.* vol. I. pp. 309-310.

is by ships from A r i a k ê and Greek ships *from Egypt*. It lies near a river at a distance from Tundis of 500 stadia, whether this is measured from river to river or by the length of the sea

---

spoken" (p. 95). From Ptolemy we learn that the capital of this prince was K a r o u r a, which has been " identified with K a r û r, an important town in the Koimbatur district originally included in the Chêra kingdom. Karûr means the black town . . Ptolemy's word K a r o u r a represents the Tamil name of the place with perfect accuracy." Nel-kunda, our author informs us, was not subject to this prince but to another called P a ḍ i ô n. This name, says Dr. Caldwell, " is of Sanskrit origin, and P a ṇ d æ, the form which Pliny, after Megas-thenes, gives in his list of the Indian nations, comes very near the Sanskrit. The more recent local information of Pliny himself, as well as the notices of Ptolemy and the *Periplûs*, supply us with the Dravidian form of the word. The Tamil sign of the masc. sing. is *an*, and Tamil inserts *i* eupho-nically after *ṇḍ*, consequently Pandiôn, and still better the plural form of the word P a ṅ d i o n e s, faithfully represents the Tamil masc. sing. *Pâṇ-ḍiyan*." In another passage the same scholar says : " The Sanskrit Paṇḍya is written in Tamil Pâṇḍiya, but the more completely tamilized form P â ṇ ḍ i is still more commonly used all over southern India. I derive Pâṇḍi, as native scholars always derive the word, from the Sanskrit Pâṇḍu, the name of the father of the Pâṇḍava brothers." The capital of this prince, as Pliny has stated, was M o d u r a, which is the Sanskrit Maṭhurâ pro-

voyage, and it is 20 stadia distant from the
mouth of its own river. The distance of N e l-
k u n d a from M o u z i r i s is also nearly 500
stadia, whether measured from river to river or

nounced in the Tamil manner. The corresponding
city in Northern India, Maṭhurâ, is written by the
Greeks M e t h o r a.

N e l k u n d a is mentioned by various authors under varying forms of the name. As has been already
stated, it is Melkunda in Ptolemy, who places it in
the country of the Aii. In the *Peutingerian Table*
it is Nincylda, and in the Geographer of Ravenna,
Nilcinna. At the mouth of the river on which
it stands was its shipping port B a k a r e or Becare,
according to Müller now represented by M a r k a r i
(lat. 12° N.) Yule conjectures that it must have
been between Kanetti and Kolum in Travancore.
Regarding the trade of this place we may quote a
remark from Vincent. " We find," he says, " that
throughout the whole which the *Periplûs* mentions
of India we have a catalogue of the exports and
imports only at the two ports of Barugaza and
Nelcynda, and there seems to be a distinction fixed
between the articles appropriate to each. Fine
muslins and ordinary cottons are the principal
commodities of the first; tortoise shell, precious
stones, silk, and above all pepper, seem to have been
procurable only at the latter. This pepper is said
to be brought to this port from Cottonara, famous
to this hour for producing the best pepper in the
world except that of Sumatra. The pre-eminence
of these two ports will account for the little that
is said of the others by the author, and why he has

by the sea voyage, but it belongs to a different kingdom, that of P a n d i ô n. It likewise is situate near a river and at about a distance from the sea of 120 stadia.

55. At the very mouth of this river lies

left us so few characters by which we may distinguish one from another."

Our author on concluding his account of Nelkunda interrupts his narrative to relate the incidents of the important discovery of the monsoon made by that Columbus of antiquity Hippalus. This account, Vincent remarks, naturally excites a curiosity in the mind to enquire how it should happen that the monsoon should have been noticed by Nearkhos, and that from the time of his voyage for 300 years no one should have attempted a direct course till Hippalus ventured to commit himself to the ocean. He is of opinion that there was a direct passage by the monsoons both in going to and coming from India in use among the Arabians before the Greeks adopted it, and that Hippalus frequenting these seas as a pilot or merchant, had met with Indian or Arabian traders who made their voyages in a more compendious manner than the Greeks, and that he collected information from them which he had both the prudence and courage to adopt, just as Columbus, while owing much to his own nautical experience and fortitude was still under obligations to the Portuguese, who had been resolving the great problems in the art of navigation for almost a century previous to his expedition.

(55) N e l k u n d a appears to have been the

another village, B a k a r ê, to which the ships despatched from Nelkunda come down *empty* and ride at anchor off shore while taking in cargo : for the river, it may be noted, has sunken reefs and shallows which make its navigation difficult. The sign by which those who come hither by sea know they are nearing land is their meeting with snakes, which are here of a black colour, not so long as those already mentioned, like serpents about the head, and with eyes the colour of blood.

56. The ships which frequent these ports are of a large size, on account of the great amount and bulkiness of the pepper and betel of which their lading consists. The imports here are principally—

Χρήματα πλεῖστα—Great quantities of specie.

Χρυσόλιθα—(Topaz ?) Gold-stone, Chrysolite.

'Ιματισμὸς ἁπλοῦς οὐ πολὺς—A small assortment of plain cloth.

Πολύμιτα—Flowered robes.

Στίμμι, κοράλλιον—Stibium, a pigment for the eyes, coral.

῞υαλος ἀργὴ χαλκὸς—White glass, copper or brass.

Κασσίτερος, μόλυβδος—Tin, lead.

Οἶνος οὐ πολύς, ὡσεὶ δὲ τοσοῦτον ὅσον ἐν Βαρυγάζοις —Wine but not much, but about as much as at Barugaza.

---

limit of our author's voyage along the coast of India, for in the sequel of his narrative he defines but vaguely the situation of the places which he

Σανδαράκη—Sandarach (*Sindúrá*).

'Αρσενικὸν—Arsenic (Orpiment), yellow sulphuret of arsenic.

Σῖτος ὅσος ἀρκέσει τοῖς περὶ το ναυκλήριον, διὰ τὸ μὴ τοὺς ἐμπόρους αὐτῷ χρῆσθαι—Corn, only for the use of the ship's company, as the merchants do not sell it.

The following commodities are brought to it for export:—

Πέπερι μονογενῶς ἐν ἑνὶ τόπῳ τούτων τῶν ἐμπορίων γεννώμενον πολύ τῇ λεγομενῃ Κοττοναρικῇ—Pepper in great quantity, produced in only one of these marts, and called the pepper of Kottonara.

Μαργαρίτης ἱκανὸς καὶ διάφορος—Pearls in great quantity and of superior quality.

'Ελέφας—Ivory.

'Οθόνια Σηρικὰ—Fine silks.

Νάρδος ἡ Γαγγητικὴ—Spikenard from the Ganges.

Μαλάβαθρον—Betel—all brought from countries further east.

Λιθία διαφανὴς παντοία—Transparent or precious stones of all sorts.

Αδάμας—Diamonds.

'Υάκινθος—Jacinths.

Χελώνη ἥτε Χρυσονησιωτικὴ καὶ ἡ περὶ τὰς νήσους θηρευομένη τὰς προκειμένας αὐτῆς τῆς Λιμυρικῆς—Tortoise-shell from the Golden Island, and another sort which is taken in the islands which lie off the coast of Limuriké.

The proper season to set sail from Egypt for

notices, while his details are scanty, and sometimes grossly inaccurate. Thus he makes the Malabar Coast extend southwards beyond Cape Comorin

r

this part of India is about the month of July—that is, Epiphi.

57. The whole round of the voyage from K a n ê and E u d a i m ô n A r a b i a, which we have just described, used to be performed in small vessels which kept close to shore and followed its windings, but H i p p a l o s was the pilot who first, by observing the bearings of the ports and the configuration of the sea, discovered the direct course across the ocean ; whence as, at the season when our own Etesians are blowing, a periodical wind from the ocean likewise blows in the Indian Sea, this wind, which is the south-west, is, it seems, called in these seas Hippalos [after the name of the pilot who first discovered the *passage by means of it*]. From the time of this discovery to the present day, merchants who sail for India either from K a n ê, or, as others do, from A r ô m a t a, if Limurikê be their destination, must often change their tack, but if they are bound for B a r u- g a z a and S k y t h i a, they are not retarded for more than three days, after which, committing themselves to the monsoon which blows right in the direction of their course, they stand far out to sea, leaving all the gulfs we have mentioned in the distance.

as far at least as Kolkhoi (near Tutikorin) on the Coromandel coast, and like many ancient writers, represents Ceylon as stretching westward almost as far as Africa.

"1. Red Bluffs at Varkkallai, in Travancore." JRAS. 1913 132.

139

58. After B a k a r ê occurs the mountain called Pyrrhos (or the Red) towards the south, near another district of the country called P a r a l i a (where the pearl-fisheries are which belong to king Pandiôn), and a city of the name of K o l k h o i . In this tract the first place met with is called B a l i t a, which has a good harbour and a village on its shore. Next to this is another place called K o m a r, where is the cape of the same name and a haven. Those who wish to consecrate the closing part of their lives to religion come hither and bathe and engage themselves to celibacy. This is also done by women; since it is related that the

---

(58) The first place mentioned after B a k a r e is P u r r h o s, or the Red Mountain, which extends along a district called P a r a l i a. "There are," says Dr. Caldwell (Introd. p. 99), "three Paralias mentioned by the Greeks, two by Ptolemy . . . one by the author of the *Periplûs.* The Paralia mentioned by the latter corresponded to Ptolemy's country of the Ἄιοι, and that of the Καρεοι, that is, to South Travancore and South Tinnevelly. It commenced at the Red Cliffs south of Quilon, and included not only Cape Comorin but also Κόλχοι, where the pearl fishing was carried on, which belonged to King Pandion. Dr. Burnell identifies Paralia with Parali, which he states is an old name for Travancore, but I am not quite able to adopt this view." "Paralia," he adds afterwards, "may possibly have corresponded in meaning, if not in sound, to some native word

See Yule's Marco Polo II p. 360

- the Chola lead in Cholamandalam. JRAS

Aroelva ... P 140, = ... Vanun ... 132

goddess (*Kumárí*) once on a time resided at the
place and bathed. From K o m a r e i (towards the
south) the country extends as far as K o l k h o i,
where the fishing for pearls is carried on.
Condemned criminals are employed in this service. King Pandión is the owner of the fishery.
To K o l k h o i succeeds another coast lying
along a gulf having a district in the interior
bearing the name of A r g a l o u. In this single
place are obtained the pearls collected near the
island of E p i o d ô r o s. From it are exported
the muslins called *ebargareitides*.

60. Among the marts and anchorages along
this shore to which merchants from Limuriké

---

meaning coast,—viz., Karei." On this coast is a
place called B a l i t a, which is perhaps the B a m-
m a l a of Ptolemy (VII. i. 9), which Mannert identifies with Manpalli, a little north of Anjenga.

(60) We now reach the great promontory called
in the *Periplûs* K o m a r and K o m a r e i, Cape
Kumari. "It has derived its name," says Caldwell, "from the Sans. *Kumárí*, a virgin, one of the
names of the goddess Durgâ, the presiding divi-
nity of the place, but the shape which this
word has taken is, especially in *komar*, distinc-
tively Tamilian." In ordinary Tamil *Kumárí*
becomes *Kumări*; and in the vulgar dialect
of the people residing in the neighbourhood of
the Cape a virgin is neither Kumárí nor Kumări
but Kŭmăr pronounced Kŏmăr. It is remarkable
that this vulgar corruption of the Sanskrit is
identical with the name given to the place by the

and the north resort, the most conspicuous are
Kamara and Podoukê and Sôpatma,
which occur in the order in which we have
named them. In these marts are found those
native vessels for coasting voyages which trade
as far as Limurikê, and another kind called

---

author of the *Periplûs* ... The monthly bathing in
honor of the goddess Durgâ is still continued at
Cape Comorin, but is not practised to the same
extent as in ancient times ... Through the continued encroachments of the sea, the harbour the
Greek mariners found at Cape Comorin and the
fort (if φρουριον is the correct reading for βριάριον
of the MS.) have completely disappeared; but a
fresh water well remains in the centre of a rock, a
little way out at sea. Regarding Kolkhoi, the
next place mentioned after Komari, the same
authority as we have seen places it (*Ind. Ant.* vol.
VI. p. 80) near Tuticorin. It is mentioned by
Ptolemy and in the *Peutinger Tables,* where it is
called 'Colcis Indorum'. The Gulf of Manaar was
called by the Greeks the Colchic Gulf. The Tamil
name of the place Kolkei is almost identical with
the Greek. "The place," according to Caldwell, "is
now about three miles inland, but there are abundant traces of its having once stood on the coast, and
I have found the tradition that it was once the seat
of the pearl fishery, still surviving amongst its inhabitants. After the sea had retired from Κόλχοι...
a new emporium arose on the coast. This was
Kâ·yal, the Cael of Marco Polo. Kâyal in turn
became in time too far from the sea .. and Tuticorin (Tûttrukuḍi) was raised instead by the

sangara, made by fastening together large vessels formed each of a single timber, and also others called *kolandiophônta*, which are of great bulk and employed for voyages to K h r u s ê and the G a n g e s. These marts import all the commodities which reach Limurikê for com-

.Portuguese from the position of a fishing village to that of the most important port on the southern Coromandel coast. The identification of Kolkoi with Kolkei is one of much importance. Being perfectly certain it helps forward other identifications. *Kol.* in Tamil means 'to slay.' *Kei* is 'hand.' It was the first capital of Pandion.

The coast beyond K o l k h o i, which has an inland district belonging to it called A r g a l o u, is indented by a gulf called by Ptolemy the Argarik—now Palk Bay. Ptolemy mentions also a promontory called Kôru and beyond it a city called A r g e i r o u and an emporium called S a l o u r. This Kôru of Ptolemy, Caldwell thinks, represents the K ô l i s of the geographers who preceded him, and the K o ṭ i of Tamil, and identifies it with "the island promontory of R â m e ś v a r a m, the point of land from which there was always the nearest access from Southern India to Ceylon." An island occurs in these parts, called that of E p i o d ô r o s, noted for its pearl fishery, on which account Ritter would identify it with the island of Manaar, which Ptolemy, as Mannert thinks, speaks of as Ναυιγηρίς (VII. i. 95). Müller thinks, however, it may be compared with Ptolemy's K ô r u, and so be Râmêśvaram.

This coast has commercial intercourse not only

mercial purposes, absorbing likewise nearly
every species of goods brought from Egypt,
and most descriptions of all the goods exported from Limuriké and disposed of on this
coast *of India.*

61. Near the region which succeeds, where

---

with the Malabar ports, but also with the Ganges
and the Golden Khersonese. For the trade with
the former a species of canoes was used called
Sangara. The Malayâlam name of these, Caldwell
says, is *Changádam,* in Tulu *Jangdla,* compare
Sanskrit *Samghddam* a raft (*Ind. Ant.* vol. I.
p. 309). The large vessels employed for the
Eastern trade were called *Kolandiophonta,* a name
which Caldwell confesses his inability to explain.

Three cities and ports are named in the order of
their occurrence which were of great commercial
importance, K a m a r a, P o d o u k e, and S o p a t-
m a. K a m a r a may perhaps be, as Müller thinks,
the emporium which Ptolemy calls K h a b ê r i s,
situated at the mouth of the River K h a b ê r o s
(now, the Kavery), perhaps, as Dr. Burnell suggests, the modern Kaveripattam. (*Ind. Ant.* vol.
VII. p. 40). P ô d o u k ê appears in Ptolemy as
Podouké. It is P u d u c h c h ê r i, *i. e.* 'new
town,' now well known as Pondicherry; so Bohlen,
Ritter, and Benfey. [Yule and Lassen place it at
Pulikât]. S o p a t m a is not mentioned in
Ptolemy, nor can it now be traced. In Sanskrit
it transliterates into *Su-patna, i. e.,* fair town.

(61) The next place noticed is the Island of
Ceylon, which is designated P a l a i s i m o u n-
d o u, with the remark that its former name was

the course of the voyage now bends to the east,
there lies out in the open sea stretching towards
the west the island now called P a l a i s i-
m o u n d o u, but by the ancients T a p r o-
b a n ê. To cross over to the northern side
of it takes a day. In the south part it gradually stretches towards the west till it nearly
reaches the opposite coast of A z a n i a. It produces pearl, precious (*transparent*) stones,
muslins, and tortoise-shell.

62. (*Returning to the coast*,) not far from the

T a p r o b a n ê. This is the Greek transliteration of
Tâmraparnî, the name given by a band of colonists
from Magadha to the place where they first
landed in Ceylon, and which was afterwards extended to the whole island. It is singular, Dr.
Caldwell remarks, that this is also the name of
the principal river in Tinnevelly on the opposite
coast of India, and he infers that the colony
referred to might previously have formed a settlement in Tinnevelly at the mouth of the Tâmra-
parṇi river—perhaps at Kolkei, the earliest residence of the Pâṇdya kings. The passage in the
Periplûs which refers to the island is very corrupt.

(62) Recurring to the mainland, the narrative notices a district called M a s a l i a, where
great quantities of cotton were manufactured.
This is the M a ï s ô l i a of Ptolemy, the region in
which he places the mouths of a river the M a i s ô-
l o s, which Benfey identifies with the Godâvarî,
in opposition to others who would make it the
Krishnâ, which is perhaps Ptolemy's T u n a. The

three marts we have mentioned lies M a s a l i a, the seaboard of a country extending far inland. Here immense quantities of fine muslins are manufactured. From M a s a l i a the course of the voyage lies eastward across a neighbouring bay to D ê s a r ê n ê, which has the breed of elephants called Bôsarê. Leaving D ê s a r ê n ê the course is northerly, passing a variety of barbarous tribes, among which are the K i r r h a- d a i, savages whose noses are flattened to the face, and another tribe, that of the B a r g u s o i,

---

name Maisôlia is taken from the Sanskrit Mausala, preserved in Machhlipatana, now Masulipatam. Beyond this, after an intervening gulf running eastward is crossed, another district occurs, D e s- a r ê n ê, noted for its elephants. This is not men- tioned by Ptolemy, but a river with a similar name, the D ô s a r ô n, is found in his enumeration of the rivers which occur between the Maisôlos and the Ganges. As it is the last in the list it may probably be, as Lassen supposes, the Brâhmini. Our author however places Desarênê at a much greater distance from the Ganges, for he peoples the intermediate space with a variety of tribes which Ptolemy relegates to the East of the river. The first of these tribes is that of the K i r r â d a i (Sanskrit, Kirâtas), whose features are of the Mongolian type. Next are the B a r g u s o i, not mentioned by Ptolemy, but perhaps to be identi- fied with the cannibal race he speaks of, the B a r o u s a i thought by Yule to be possibly the inhabitants of the Nikobar islands, and lastly the

as well as the Hîppioprosôpoi *or* Ma-
kroprosôpoi (the horse faced or long faced
men), who are reported to be cannibals.

63. After passing these, the course turns
again to the east, and if you sail with the ocean
to your right and the coast far to your left, you
reach the Ganges and the extremity of the continent towards the east *called* Khrusê (the
Golden Khersonese). The river of this region
called the Ganges is the largest in India;
it has an *annual* increase and decrease like the
Nile, and there is on it a mart called after it,
Gangê, through which passes *a considerable
traffic* consisting of betel, the Gangetic spike-

---

tribe of the long or horse-faced men who were also
cannibals.

(63) When this coast of savages and monsters
is left behind, the course lies eastward, and leads
to the Ganges, which is the greatest river of
India, and adjoins the extremity of the Eastern
continent called Khrusê, or the Golden. Near
the river, or, according to Ptolemy, on the third of
its mouths stands a great emporium of trade
called Gangê, exporting *Malabathrum* and cottons and other commodities. Its exact position
there are not sufficient data to determine. Khrusê
is not only the name of the last part of the continent, but also of an island lying out in the ocean
to eastward, not far from the Ganges. It is the
last part of the world which is said to be inhabited.
The situation of Khrusê is differently defined by
different ancient authors. It was not known to

nard, pearl, and the finest of all muslins—those called the Gangetic. In this locality also there is said to be a gold mine and a gold coin called *Kaltis*. Near this river there is an island of the ocean called K h r u s ê (or the Golden), which lies directly under the rising sun and at the extremity of the world towards the east. It produces the finest tortoise-shell that is found throughout the whole of the Erythræan Sea.

64. Beyond this region, immediately under the north, where the sea terminates outwards, there lies somewhere in T h î n a a very great city,—not on the coast, but in the interior of the country, called T h î n a,—from which silk, whether in the raw state or spun into thread

---

the Alexandrine geographers. Pliny seems to have preserved the most ancient report circulated regarding it. He says (VI. xxiii. 80) : " Beyond the mouth of the Indus are C h r y s ê and A r g y r e abounding in metals as I believe, for I can hardly credit what some have related that the soil consists of gold and silver." Mela (III. 7) assigns to it a very different position, asserting it to be near T a b i s, the last spur of the range of Taurus. He therefore places it where Eratosthenês places T h î n a i, to the north of the Ganges on the confines of the Indian and Skythian oceans. Ptolemy, in whose time the Transgangetic world was better known, refers it to the peninsula of Malacca, the Golden Khersonese.

(64) The last place which the *Periplûs* mentions is Thinai, an inland city of the T h i n a i or

and woven into cloth, is brought by land to
Barugaza through Baktria, or by the Ganges to
Limurikê. To penetrate into T h î n a is not
an easy undertaking, and but few *merchants*
come from it, and that rarely. Its situation is
under the Lesser Bear, and it is said to be con-
terminous with the remotest end of Pontos,
and that part of the Kaspian Sea which adjoins
the Maiôtic Lake, along with which it issues by
one and the same mouth into the ocean.

65. On the confines, however, of T h î n a i
an annual fair is held, attended by a race of men
of squat figure, with their face very broad, but
mild in disposition, called the S ê s a t a i, who in
appearance resemble wild animals. They come
with their wives and children to this fair, bringing heavy loads of goods wrapped up in mats
resembling in outward appearance the early
leaves of the vine. Their place of assembly is
where their own territory borders with that of
Thinai; and here, squatted on the mats on which

S i n a i, having a large commerce in silk and
woollen stuffs. The ancient writers are not at all
agreed as to its position, Colonel Yule thinks it
was probably the city described by Marco Polo
under the name of K e n j a n-f u (that is Si-
ngan-fu or Chauggan,) the most celebrated city
in Chinese history, and the capital of several of
the most potent dynasties. It was the metropolis of Shi Hwangti of the T'Sin dynasty, properly the first emperor, and whose conquests almost

they exhibit their wares, they feast for several days, after which they return to their homes in the interior.   On observing their retreat the people of Thinai, repairing to the spot, collect the mats on which they had been sitting, and taking out the fibres, which are called *petroi*, from the reeds, they put the leaves two and two together, and roll them up into slender balls, through which they pass the fibres extracted from the reeds. 'Three kinds of Malabathrum are thus made—that of the large ball, that of the middle, and that of the small, according to the size of the leaf of which the balls are formed. Hence there are three kinds of Malabathrum, which after being made up are forwarded to India by the manufacturers.

66. All the regions beyond this are unexplored, being difficult of access by reason of the extreme rigour of the climate and the severe frosts, or perhaps because such is the will of the divine power.

intersected those of his contemporary Ptolemy Euergetês—(vide Yule's *Travels of Marco Polo*, vol. II. p. 21).

THE

VOYAGE OF NEARKHOS,

FROM THE INDUS TO THE HEAD OF THE PERSIAN GULF,

AS DESCRIBED IN THE SECOND PART OF THE INDIKA OF ARRIAN,

(FROM CHAPTER XVIII. TO THE END.)

TRANSLATED FROM MÜLLER'S EDITION

(As given in the *Geographi Græci Minores ; Paris, 1855*).

WITH INTRODUCTION AND NOTES.

THE VOYAGE OF NEARKHOS.

INTRODUCTION.

The coasting voyage from the mouth of the
Indus to the head of the Persian Gulf, designed
by Alexander the Great, and executed by Nearkhos,
may be regarded as the most important achievement of the ancients in navigation. It opened
up, as Vincent remarks, a communication between
Europe and the most distant countries of Asia,
and, at a later period, was the source and origin
of the Portuguese discoveries, and consequently
the primary cause, however remote, of the British
establishments in India. A Journal of this
voyage was written by Nearkhos himself, which,
though not extant in its original form, has been
preserved for us by Arrian, who embodied its
contents in his little work on India,[1] which he
wrote as a sequel to his history of the expedition
of Alexander.

Nearkhos as a writer must be acknowledged to
be most scrupulously honest and exact,—for the
result of explorations made in modern times
along the shores which he passed in the course
of his voyage shows that his description of them
is accurate even in the most minute particulars.
His veracity was nevertheless oppugned in ancient
times by Strabo, who unjustly stigmatises the
whole class of the Greek writers upon India as
mendacious. "Generally speaking," he says (II.
i. 9), "the men who have written upon Indian

---

[1] Written in the Ionic dialect.

t

affairs were a set of liars. Deimakhos holds the
first place in the list, Megasthenês comes next,
while Onêsikritos and Nearkhos, with others of
the same class, stammer out a few words of truth."
(παραψελλίζοντες). Strabo, however, in spite of this
censure did not hesitate to use Nearkhos as one
of his chief authorities for his description of
India, and is indebted to him for many facts relating to that country, which, however extraordinary they might appear to his contemporaries,
have been all confirmed by subsequent observa-
tion. It is therefore fairly open to doubt whether
Strabo was altogether sincere in his ill opinion,
seeing it had but little, if any, influence on his practice. We know at all events that he was too much
inclined to undervalue any writer who retailed
fables, without discriminating whether the writer
set them down as facts, or merely as stories, which
he had gathered from hearsay.

In modern times, the charge of mendacity has
been repeated by Hardouin and Huet. There are,
however, no more than two passages of the Journal
which can be adduced to support this imputa-
tion. The first is that in which the excessive
breadth of 200 stadia is given to the Indus, and
the second that in which it is asserted that at
Malana (situated in 25° 17' of N. latitude) the
shadows at noon were observed to fall southward, and this in the month of November. With
regard to the first charge, it may be supposed that
the breadth assigned to the Indus was probably
that which it was observed to have when in a
state of inundation, and with regard to the second,
it may be met by the supposition, which is quite

admissible, that Arrian may have misapprehended in some measure the import of the statement as made by Nearkhos. The passage will be afterwards examined,[*] but in the meantime we may say, with Vincent, that if the difficulty it presents admits of no satisfactory solution, the misstatement ought not, as standing alone, to be insisted upon to the invalidation of the whole work.

But another charge besides that of mendacity has been preferred against the Journal. Dodwell has denied its authenticity. His attack is based on the following passage in Pliny (VI. 23):—Onesciriti et Nearchi navigatio nec nomina habet mansionum nec spatia. *The Journal of Onesicritus and Nearchus has neither the names of the anchorages nor the measure of the distances.* From this Dodwell argues that, as the account of the voyage in Arrian contains both the names and the distances, it could not have been a transcript of the Journal of Nearkhos, which according to Pliny gave neither names nor distances. Now, in the first place, it may well be asked, why the authority of Pliny, who is by no means always a careful writer, should be set so high as to override all other testimony, for instance, that of Arrian himself, who expressly states in the outset of his narrative that he intended to give the account of the voyage which had been written by Nearkhos. In the second place, the passage in question is probably corrupt, or if not, it is in direct conflict with the passage which immediately follows it, and contains Pliny's own summary of the voyage in which little else

---

[*] See infra, note 35.

is given than the names of the anchorages and
the distances. Dodwell was aware of the inconsis-
tency of the two passages, and endeavoured to
explain it away. In this he entirely fails, and
there can therefore be no reasonable doubt, that
in Arrian's work we have a record of the voyage
as authentic as it is veracious.

Of that record we proceed to give a brief ab-
stract, adding a few particulars gathered from other
sources.

The fleet with which Nearkhos accomplished
the voyage consisted of war-galleys and transports
which had been partly built and partly collected
on the banks of the river Hydaspes (now the
Jhelam), where Alexander had supplied them with
crews by selecting from his troops such men as
had a knowledge of seamanship. The fleet thus
manned sailed slowly down the Hydaspes, the
Akesines, and the Indus, its movements being
regulated by those of the army, which, in marching
down towards the sea, was engaged in reducing the
warlike tribes settled along the banks of these
rivers. This downward voyage occupied, according
to Strabo, ten months, but it probably did not occupy more than nine. The fleet having at length
reached the apex of the Delta formed by the Indus
remained in that neighbourhood for some time at
a place called Pattala, which has generally been
identified with Thatha—a town near to where the
western arm of the Indus bifurcates,—but which
Cunningham and others would prefer to identify
with Nirankol or Haidarâbâd.[3] From Pattala

---

[3] Geog. of Anc. India, p. 279 sqq.

Alexander sailed down the western stream of the river, where some of his ships were damaged and others destroyed by encountering the Bore, a phenomenon as alarming as it was new to the Greeks.[a] He returned to Pattala, and thence made an excursion down the Eastern stream, which he found less difficult to navigate. On again returning to Pattala he removed his fleet down to a station on the Western branch of the river (at an island called Killouta),[b] which was at no great distance from the sea. He then set out on his return to Persia, leaving instructions with Nearkhos to start on the voyage as soon as the calming of the monsoon should render navigation safe. It was the king's intention to march near to the coast, and to collect at convenient stations supplies for the victualling of the fleet, but he found that such a route was impracticable, and he was obliged to lead his army through the inland provinces which lay between India and his destination, Sûsa.[c] He left Leonnatos, however, behind him in the country of the Oreitai, with instructions to render every assistance in his power to the expedition under Nearkhos when it should reach that part of the coast.

Nearkhos remained in the harbour at Killouta for about a month after Alexander had departed, and then sailed during a temporary lull in the monsoon, as he was apprehensive of being at-

---

[a] See Arrian's Anab. VI. 19. Καὶ τοῦτο οὔπω πρότερον ἐγνωκόσι τοῖς ἀμφ' Ἀλέξανδρον ἔκπληξιν μὲν καὶ αὐτὸ οὐ σμικρὰν παρέσχε.

[b] See Arrian, ib.

[c] See id. VI. 23, and Strab. xv. ii 3, 4.

tacked by the natives who had been but imperfectly
subjugated, and whose spirit was hostile.[7] The
date on which he set sail is fixed by Vincent as
the 1st of October in the year B.C. 326. He proceeded slowly down the river, and anchored first
at a place called Stoura, which was only 100 stadia
distant from the station they had quitted. Here
the fleet remained for two days, when it proceeded
to an anchorage only 30 stadia farther down the
stream at a place called Kaumana.[8] Thence
it proceeded to Koreâtis (v. l. Koreëstis)—where it
again anchored. When once more under weigh its
progress was soon arrested by a dangerous rock
or bar which obstructed the mouth of the river.[9]
After some delay this difficulty was overcome, and
the fleet was conducted in safety into the open
main, and onward to an island called Krôkala
(150 stadia distant from the bar), where it remained at anchor throughout the day following its arrival. On leaving this island Nearkhos
had Mount Eiros (now Manora) on his right hand,
and a low flat island on his left; and this, as
Cunningham remarks, is a very accurate description of the entrance to Karâchi harbour.
The fleet was conducted into this harbour, now
so well known as the great emporium of the trade
of the Indus, and here, as the monsoon was still
blowing with great violence, it remained for four
and twenty days. The harbour was so commodious
and secure that Nearkhos designated it the Port

---

[7] Strab. ib. 5.
[8] This may perhaps be represented by the modern Khâu,
the name of one of the western mouths of the Indus.
[9] See infra, p. 176, note 17.

of Alexander. It was well sheltered by an island lying close to its mouth, called by Arrian, Bibakta, but by Pliny, Bibaga, and by Philostratos, Biblos.

The expedition took its departure from this station on the 3rd of November. It suffered both from stress of weather and from shortness of provisions until it reached Kôkala on the coast of the Oreitai, where it took on board the supplies which had been collected for its use by the exertions of Leonnatos. Here it remained for about 10 days, and by the time of its departure the monsoon had settled in its favour, so that the courses daily accomplished were now of much greater length than formerly. The shores, however, of the Ikhthyophagoi, which succeeded to those of the Oreitai, were so miserably barren and inhospitable that provisions were scarcely procurable, and Nearkhos was apprehensive lest the men, famished and despairing, should desert the ships. Their sufferings were not relieved till they approached the straits, which open into the Persian Gulf. When within the straits, they entered the mouth of the river Anamis (now the Minâb or Ibrahim river), and having landed, formed a dockyard and a camp upon its banks. This place lay in Harmozeia, a most fertile and beautiful district belonging to Karmania. Nearkhos, having here learned that Alexander was not more than a 5 days' journey from the sea, proceeded into the interior to meet him, and report the safety of the expedition. During his absence the ships were repaired and provisioned, and therefore soon after his return to the camp he gave orders for the resumption of the voyage. The time spent at Har-

mozeia was one and twenty days. The fleet
again under weigh coasted the islands lying at
the mouth of the gulf, and then having shaped
its course towards the mainland, passed the
western shores of Karmania and those of Persis,
till it arrived at the mouth of the Sitakos (now the
Kara-Agach), where it was again repaired and
supplied with provisions, remaining for the same
number of days as at the Anamis. One of the
next stations at which it touched was Mesembria,
which appears to have been situated in the neighbourhood of the modern Bushire. The coast of
Persis was difficult to navigate on account of
intricate and oozy channels, and of shoals and
breakers which frequently extended far out to
sea. The coast which succeeded, that of Sousis
(from which Persis is separated by the river
Arosis or Oroâtis, now the Tâb) was equally
difficult and dangerous to navigate, and therefore the fleet no longer crept along the shore,
but stood out more into the open sea. At the
head of the gulf Sousis bends to westward,
and here are the mouths of the Tigris and
Euphrates, which appear in those days to have
entered the sea by separate channels. It was
the intention of Nearkhos to have sailed up the
former river, but he passed its mouth unawares,
and continued sailing westward till he reached
Diridôtis (or Terêdon), an emporium in Babylonia, situated on the Pallacopas branch of the
Euphrates. From Diridôtis he retraced his course,
and entering the mouth of the Tigris sailed up its
stream till he reached the lower end of a great
lake (not now existing), through which its current

flowed. At the upper end of this lake was a village called Aginis, said to have been 500 stadia distant from Sousa. Nearkhos did not, as has been erroneously supposed by some, sail up the lake to Aginis, but entered the mouth of a river which flows into its south-eastern extremity, called the Pasitigris or Eulaeus, the Ulai of the Prophet Daniel, now the Karûn. The fleet proceeded up this river, and came to a final anchor in its stream immediately below a bridge, which continued the highway from Persis to Sousa. This bridge, according to Ritter and Rawlinson, crossed the Pasitigris at a point near the modern village of Ahwaz. Here the fleet and the army were happily reunited. Alexander on his arrival embraced Nearkhos with cordial warmth, and rewarded appropriately the splendid services which he had rendered by bringing the expedition safely through so many hardships and perils to its destination. The date on which the fleet anchored at the bridge is fixed by Vincent for the 24th of February B. c. 325, so that the whole voyage was performed in 146 days, or somewhat less than 5 months.

The following tables show the names, positions, &c., of the different places which occurred on the route taken by the expedition :—

I.

From the Station on the Indus to the Port of Alexander (Karâchi Harbour).

Ancient name.	Modern name.	Distance in Stadia[10]	Lat. N.	Long. E.
1. Station at Killouta.	Near Lari-Bandar.	...	24° 30′	67° 28′
2. Stoura	....	100		
3. Kaumana ...	Khau	30		
4. Koreatis ...	....	20		
5. Herma	*Bar in the Indus.*			
6. Krôkala......	....	120		
7. *Mount Eiros.*	Manora.			
8. *Is. unnamed.*				
9. The Port of Alexander.	Karâchi ...	...	24° 53′	66° 57′

[10] The Olympic stadium, which was in general use throughout Greece, contained 600 Greek feet = 625 Roman feet, or 606¾ English feet. The Roman mile contained eight stadia, being about half a stadium less than an English mile. Not a few of the measurements given by Arrian are excessive, and it has therefore been conjectured that he may have used some standard different from the Olympic,—which, however, is hardly probable. See the subject discussed in Smith's Dictionary of Antiquities, S. V. *Stadium.*

II.

Coast of the Arabies (Sindh).

Length of the Coast from the Indus to the
Arabis R. .... 1000 Stadia.
Actual length in miles English ... 80
Time taken in its navigation ...... 38 Days.

Ancient name.	Modern name.	Distance in Stadia.	Lat. N.	Long.E.
1. Port of Alexander	Karâchi ...	...	24° 53'	66° 57
2. *Bitakta.*				
3. Domai Is. ...	....	60	24° 48'	66° 50'
4. Saranga	....	300	24° 44'	66° 34'
5. Sakala	....	...	24° 52'	66° 33'
6. Morontobara	....	300	25° 13'	66° 40'
7. *Is. unnamed.*				
8. Arabis R. ...	Purâli R...	120	25° 28'	66° 35'

III.

Coast of the Oreitai (Las.)

Length of the coast (Arrian) .... 1600 Stadia.
    Do.   do.   (Strabo) .... 1800 ,,
Actual length in miles English ....,.. 100
Time taken in its navigation .... 18 Days.

Ancient name.	Modern name.	Distance in Stadia.	Lat. N.	Long.E.
1. Pagala	....	200	25° 30'	66° 15'
2. Kabana	....	400	25° 28'	65° 46'
3. Kôkala	Near Râs-Katchari.	200	25° 21'	65° 36'
4. Toméros R. .	Maklow or HingulR.	500	25° 16'	65° 15'
5. Malana	Râs Malan.	300	25° 18'	65° 7'

IV.

Coast of the Ikhthyophagoi (Mekran or Belu-
chistan).

Length of the coast (Arrian) ....10,000 Stadia.
   Do.   do.   (Strabo) .... 7,000 „
Actual length in miles English 480
Time taken in its navigation .... 20 Days.

Ancient name.	Modern name.	Distance in Stadia.	Lat. N.	Long.E.
1. Bagisara ...	On Arabah or Hor-maraBay	600	25° 12'	64° 31'
2. *Pasira*				
3. Cape unnamed.	Râs Arabah	...	25° 7'	64° 29'
4. Kolta	... .	200	25° 8'	64° 27'
5. Kalama	Kalami R..	600	25° 21'	63° 59'
6. *Karbine Is.* .	Asthola or Sangâ-dîp			
7. Kissa in *Karbis.*	....	200	25° 22'	63° 37'
8. Cape unnamed.	C. Passence..	...	25° 15'	63° 30'
9. Mosarna ...	Near do.			
10. Balômon ...	....	750		
11. Barna.........	....	400	25° 12'	63° 10'
12. Dendrobôsa .	Daram or Duram.	200	25° 11'	62° 45'
13. Kôphas	Râs Koppa	400	25° 11'	62° 29'
14. Kuiza.........	Near Râs Ghunse.	800	25° 10'	61° 56'
15. Town un-named.	OnGwattar Bay.	500		
16. Cape called Bagia.	....	...	25° 7'	61° 28'
17. Talmena ...	On Chau-bar Bay.	1000	25° 24'	60° 40'
18. Kanasis......	....	400	25° 24'	60° 12'

Ancient name.	Modern name.	Distance in Stadia.	Lat. N.	Long.E.
19. Anchorage unnamed.				
20. Kanate	Kungoun..	850	25° 25′	59° 15
21. Taœi orTroi-si.	Near Su-dich River.	800	25° 30′	58° 42
22. Bagasira ...	Girishk ...	300	25° 38′	58° 27′
23. Anchorage unnamed.	....	1100		

V

Coast of Karmania (Moghistan and Laristan).

Length of the coast (Arrian and Strabo) .... 3,700 Stadia.

Actual length in miles English.. 296

Time taken in its navigation ... 19 Days.

Ancient name.	Modern name.	Distance in Stadia.	Lat. N.	Long.E.
1. Anchorage unnamed.				
2. Badis.........	Near Cape Bombarek	...	25° 47′	57° 48
3. Anchorage unnamed.	....	800		
4. Cape Maketa in Arabia..	Cape Mu-sendom.			
5. Neoptana ...	Nr. Karun.	700	26° 57′	57° 1′
6. Anamis R....	Mînâb R..	100	27° 11′	57° 6′
7. Organa Is. .	Ormus or Djerun.			
8. Oarakta Is. 2 anchorages	Kishm ...	300		

Ancient name.	Modern name.	Distance in Stadia.	Lat. N.	Long.E.
9. *Island dist. from it 40 stadia.*	*Angar or Hanjam.*			
10. Island 300 stadia from mainland.	Tombo......	400	26° 20′	55° 20′
11. *Pylora Is.* ...	*Polior Is.* .	...	26° 20′	54° 35′
12. Sisidônê ...	Mogos ? ...			
13. Tarsia	C. Djard...	300	26° 20′	54° 21′
14. Kataia Is. ...	Kenn	300	26° 32′	54°

VI.

Coast of Persis (Farsistan).

Length of Coast ....4,400 Stadia.
Actual length in miles English ... 382
Time taken in its navigation:........ 31 Days.

Ancient name.	Modern name.	Distance in Stadia.	Lat. N.	Long.E.
1. Ila and Kaïkander Is..	Inderabia Island.	400	26° 38′	53° 35′
2. Island with PearlFishery.				
3. Another anchorage here.	....	40		
4. MountOkhos	....	...	26° 59′	53° 20′
5. Apostana. ...	....	450	27° 1′	52° 55′
6. Bay unnamed.	On it is Nabend.	400	27° 24′	52° 25′
7. Gogana at mouth of Areon R.	Konkan ...	600	27° 48′	52°

Ancient name.	Modern name.	Distance in Stadia.	Lat. N.	Long. E.
8. Sitakos	Kara-Agach R.	800		
9. Hieratis......	....	750	28° 52'	50° 45'
10. HeratemisR. near it.				
11. Podagron, R.				
12. Mesambria. .	Near Bu-shire.	...	29°	50° 45'
13. Taökê on Granis, R.	Taaug	200	29° 14'	50° 30'
14. Rhogonis, R.	....	200	29° 27'	50° 29'
15. Brizana, R. .	....	400	29° 57'	50° 15'
16. Arosis or Oroatis, R.	River Tâb.	...	30° 4'	49° 30'

VII.

Coast of Sousis (Khuzistan.)

Length of the Coast..................... 2000 Stadia.

Time taken in its navigation .... 3 Days.

Ancient name.	Modern name.	Distance in Stadia.	Lat. N.	Long E.
1. Kataderbis R.	....	500	30° 16'	49°
2. MargastanaIs				
3. Anchorage unnamed.	....	600		
4. Diridôtis,the end of the sea voyage.	Near Jebel Sanâm.	900	30° 12'	47° 35'

XVIII. When the fleet formed for Alexander upon the banks of the Hydaspes was now ready, he provided crews for the vessels by collecting all the Phœnikians and all the Kyprians and Egyptians who had followed him in his Eastern campaigns, and from these he selected such as were skilled in seamanship to manage the vessels and work the oars. He had besides in his army not a few islanders familiar with that kind of work, and also natives both of Ionia and of the Hellespont. The following officers he appointed as Commanders of the different galleys[11] :—

Makedonians.

Citizens of Pella.

1. Hephaistiôn, son of Amyntor.
2. Leonnatos, son of Anteas.
3. Lysimakhos, son of Agathoklês.
4. Asklepiodôros, son of Timander.
5. Arkhôn, son of Kleinias.

---

[11] This list does not specify those officers who performed the voyage, but such as had a temporary command during the passage down the river. The only names which occur afterwards in the narrative are those of Arkhias and Onêsikritos. Nearkhos, by his silence, leaves it uncertain whether any other officers enumerated in his list accompanied him throughout the expedition. The following are known not to have done so: Hephaistion, Leonnatos, Lysimakhos, Ptolemy, Krateros, Attalos and Peukestas. It does not clearly appear what number of ships or men accompanied Nearkhos to the conclusion of the voyage. If we suppose the ships of war only fit for the service, 30 galleys might possibly contain from two to three thousand men, but this estimation is uncertain.
See Vincent, I. 118 sqq.

6. Demonikos, son of Athenaios.
7. Arkhias, son of Anaxidotos.
8. Ophellas, son of Seilênos.
9. Timanthês, son of Pantiadês.
    Of Amphipolis.
10. Nearkhos, son of Androtîmos, who wrote a narrative of the voyage.
11. Laomedôn, son of Larikhos.
12. Androsthenês, son of Kallistratos.
    Of Oresis.
13. Krateros, son of Alexander.
14. Perdikkas, son of Orontes.
    Of Eördaia.
15. Ptolemaios, son of Lagos.
16. Aristonous, son of Peisaios.
    Of Pydna.
17. Metrôn, son of Epikharmos.
18. Nikarkhidês, son of Simos.
    Of Stymphaia.
19. Attalos, son of Andromenês.
    Of Mieza.
20. Peukestas, son of Alexander.
    Of Alkomenai.
21. Peithôn, son of Krateuas.
    Of Aigai.
22. Leonnatos, son of Antipater.
    Of Alôros.
23. Pantoukhos, son of Nikolaös.
    Of Beroia.
24. Mylleas, son of Zôilos.
    All these were Makedonians.
    Greeks,—of Larisa :
25. Mêdios, son of Oxynthemis.
    Of Kardia.

26. Eumenês, son of Hierônymos.
    Of Kôs.
27. Kritoboulos, son of Plato.
    Of Magnêsia :
28. Thoas, son of Mênodôros.
29. Maiandor, son of Mandrogenês.
    Of Teos :
30. Andrôn, son of Kabêlas.
    Of Soloi in Cyprus :
31. Nikokleês, son of Pasikratês.
    Of Salamis in Cyprus :
32. Nithaphôn, son of Pnutagoras.
A Persian was also appointed as a Trierarch :
33. Bagoas, son of Pharnoukhês.

The Pilot and Master of Alexander's own ship
was Onêsikritos of Astypalaia, and the Secretary-
General of the fleet Euagoras, the son of Eukleôn,
a Corinthian. Nearkhos, the son of Androtìmos,
a Kretan by birth, but a citizen of Amphipolis on
the Strymôn was appointed as Admiral of the
expedition.

When these dispositions had been all completed,
Alexander sacrificed to his ancestral gods, and to
such as had been indicated by the oracle; also to
Poseidôn and Amphitritê and the Nêreids, and to
Okeanos himself, and to the River Hydaspês, from
which he was setting forth on his enterprise; and
to the Akesinês into which the Hydaspês pours its
stream, and to the Indus which receives both
these rivers. He further celebrated the occasion
by holding contests in music and gymnastics,
and by distributing to the whole army, rank by
rank, the sacrificial victims.

XIX. When all the preparations for the voyage

had been made, Alexander ordered Krateros, with a force of horse and foot, to go to one side of the Hydaspês; while Hephaistiôn commanding a still larger force, which included 200 elephants, should march in a parallel line on the other side. Alexander himself had under his immediate command the body of foot guards called the Hypaspists, and all the archers, and what was called the companion-cavalry,—a force consisting in all of 8,000 men. The troops under Krateros and Hephaistiôn marching in advance of the fleet had received instructions where they were to wait its arrival. Philip, whom he had appointed satrap of this region, was despatched to the banks of the Akesinês with another large division, for by this time he had a following of 120,000 soldiers,[12] including those whom he had himself led up from the sea-coast, as well as the recruits enlisted by the agents whom he had deputed to collect an army, when he admitted to his ranks barbarous tribes of all countries in whatever way they might be armed. Then weighing anchor, he sailed down the Hydaspês to its point of junction with the Akesinês. The ships numbered altogether 1800, including the long narrow war galleys, the round-shaped roomy merchantmen, and the transports for carrying horses and provisions to feed the army. But how the fleet sailed down the rivers, and what tribes Alexander conquered in the course of the voyage, and how he was in danger among the Malli,[13] and

[12] So also Plutarch in the Life of Alexander (C.66) says that in returning from India Alexander had 120,000 foot and 15,000 cavalry.
[13] Sansk. Malava. The name is preserved in the modern Moultan.

how he was wounded in their country, and how Peukestas and Leonnatos covered him with their shields when he fell,—all these incidents have been already related in my other work, that which is written in the Attic dialect.[14] My present object is to give an account of the coasting voyage which Nearkhos accomplished with the fleet when starting from the mouths of the Indus he sailed through the great ocean as far as the Persian Gulf, called by some the Red Sea.

XX. Nearkhos himself has supplied a narrative of this voyage, which runs to this effect. Alexander, he informs us, had set his heart on navigating the whole circuit of the sea which extends from India to Persia, but the length of the voyage made him hesitate, and the possibility of the destruction of his fleet, should it be cast on some desert coast either quite harbourless or too barren to furnish adequate supplies; in which case a great stain tarnishing the splendour of his former actions would obliterate all his good fortune. His ambition, however, to be always doing something new and astonishing prevailed over all his scruples. Then arose a difficulty as to what commander he should choose, having genius sufficient for working out his plans, and a difficulty also with regard to the men on ship-board how he could overcome their fear, that in being despatched on such a service they were recklessly sent into open peril. Nearkhos here tells us that Alexander consulted him on the choice of a commander, and that when the king had mentioned

---

[14] Anab. VI. 11.

one man after another, rejecting all, some because they were not inclined to expose themselves for his sake to danger, others because they were of a timid temper, others because their only thought was how to get home, making this and that objection to each in turn, Nearkhos then proffered his own services in these terms: "I, then, O king, engage to command the expedition, and, under the divine protection, will conduct the fleet and the people on board safe into Persia, if the sea be that way navigable, and the undertaking within the power of man to perform." Alexander made a pretence of refusing the offer, saying that he could not think of exposing any friend of his to the distresses and hazard of such a voyage, but Nearkhos, so far from withdrawing his proposal, only persisted the more in pressing its acceptance upon him. Alexander, it need not be said, warmly appreciated the promptitude to serve him shown by Nearkhos, and appointed him to be commander-in-chief of the expedition. When this became known, it had a great effect in calming the minds of the troops ordered on this service and on the minds of the sailors, since they felt assured that Alexander would never have sent forth Nearkhos into palpable danger unless their lives were to be preserved. At the same time the splendour with which the ships were equipped, and the enthusiasm of the officers vying with each other who should collect the best men, and have his complement most effective, inspired even those who had long hung back with nerve for the work, and a good hope that success would crown the undertaking. It added to the cheer-

fulness pervading the army that Alexander himself sailed out from both the mouths of the Indus
into the open main when he sacrificed victims to
Poseidôn and all the other sea-deities, and presented gifts of great magnificence to the sea; and
so the men trusting to the immeasurable good
fortune which had hitherto attended all the projects
of Alexander, believed there was nothing he might
not dare—nothing but would to him be feasible.

XXI. When the Etesian winds,[15] which continue all the hot season blowing landward from
the sea, making navigation on that coast impracticable, had subsided, then the expedition
started on the voyage in the year when Kephisidôros was Archon at Athens, on the 20th
day of the month Boëdromion according to the
Athenian Kalendar, but as the Makedonians and
Asiatics reckon * * in the 11th year of the
reign of Alexander.[16] Nearkhos, before putting to

---

[15] The general effect of the monsoon Nearkhos certainly
knew; he was a native of Crete, and a resident at
Amphipolis, both which lie within the track of the annual
or Etesian winds, which commencing from the Hellespont
and probably from the Euxine sweep the Egêan sea, and
stretching quite across the Mediterranean to the coast of
Africa, entered through Egypt to Nubia or Ethiopia. Arrian
has accordingly mentioned the monsoon by the name of
the Etesian winds; his expression is remarkable, and attended with a precision that does his accuracy credit. These
Etesian winds, says he, do not blow from the north in the
summer months as with us in the Mediterranean, but from
the South. On the commencement of winter, or at latest
on the setting of the Pleiades, the sea is said to be navigable
till the winter solstice (Anab. VI. 21-1) Vincent I. 43 sq.

[16] The date here fixed by Arrian is the 2nd of October
326 B.C., but the computation now generally accepted
refers the event to the year after to suit the chronology of
Alexander's subsequent history (see Clinton's F. Hell. II.
pp. 174 and 563, 3rd ed.). There was an Archon called

sea sacrifices to Zeus the Preserver, and celebrates,
as Alexander had done, gymnastic games. Then
clearing out of harbour they end the first day's
voyage by anchoring in the Indus at a creek called
Stoura, where they remain for two days. The
distance of this place from the station they had-
just left was 100 stadia. On the third day they
resumed the voyage, but proceeded no further
than 30 stadia, coming to an anchor at another
creek, where the water was now salt, for the sea
when filled with the tide ran up the creek, and
its waters even when the tide receded commingled
with the river. The name of this place was Kaumana. The next day's course, which was of 20
stadia only, brought them to Korcätis, where they
once more anchored in the river. When again
under weigh their progress was soon interrupted,
for a bar was visible which there obstructed the
mouth of the Indus; and the waves were heard
breaking with furious roar upon its strand which
was wild and rugged. Observing, however, that
the bar at a particular part was soft, they made a
cutting through this, 5 stadia long, *at low water*,
and on the return of the flood-tide carried the
ships through by the passage thus formed into the

Kephisidoros in office in the year B.C. 323-322; so Arrian
has here either made a mistake, or perhaps an Archon of
the year 326-325 may have died during his tenure of office,
and a substitute called Kephisidôros been elected to fill the
vacancy. The *lacuna* marked by the asterisks has been
supplied by inserting the name of the Makedonian mouth
Dius. The Ephesians adopted the names of the months
used by the Makedonians, and so began their year with the
month Dius, the first day of which corresponds to the 24th
of September. The 20th day of Boedromion of the year
B.C. 325 corresponded to the 21st of September.

open sea.[17] Then following the winding of the coast
they ran a course of 120 stadia, and reach Krôkala,[18]

[17] Regarding the sunken reef encountered by the fleet after
leaving Koreatis, Sir Alexander Burnes says: "Near the
mouth of the river we passed a rock stretching across the
stream, which is particularly mentioned by Nearchus, who
calls it *a dangerous rock*, and is the more remarkable since
there is not even a stone below Tatta in any other part of
the Indus." The rock, he adds, is at a distance of six miles
up the Pitti. "It is vain," says Captain Wood in the
narrative of his *Journey to the Source of the Oxus*, " in
the delta of such a river (as the Indus), to identify existing
localities with descriptions handed down to us by the historians of Alexander the Great. . . . . (but) Burnes has, I
think, shown that the mouth by which the Grecian fleet
left the Indus was the modern Piti. The 'dangerous
rock' of Nearchus completely identifies the spot, and as
it is still in existence, without any other within a circle of
many miles, we can wish for no stronger evidence." With
regard to the canal dug through this rock, Burnes remarks :
" The Greek admiral only availed himself of the experience
of the people, for it is yet customary among the natives of
Sind to dig shallow canals, and leave the tides or river to
deepen them ; and a distance of five stadia, or half a mile,
would call for not great labour. It is not to be supposed
that sandbanks will continue unaltered for centuries, but
I may observe that there was a large bank contiguous to
the island, between it and which a passage like that of
Nearchus might have been dug with the greatest advantage." The same author thus describes the mouth of the
Piti :—" Beginning from the westward we have the Pitti
mouth, an embouchure of the Buggaur, that falls into what
may be called the Bay of Karâchi. It has no bar, but a
large sandbank, together with an island outside prevent a
direct passage into it from the sea, and narrow the channel
to about half a mile at its mouth."

[18] All inquirers have agreed in identifying the Kolaka
of Ptolemy, and the sandy island of Krokola where Nearchus tarried with his fleet for one day, with a small island
in the bay of Karâchi. Krokala is further described as
lying off the mainland of the Arabii. It was 150 stadia,
or 17¼ miles, from the western mouth of the Indus,—which
agrees exactly with the relative positions of Karâchi and
the mouth of the Ghâra river, if, as we may fairly assume,
the present coast-line has advanced five or six miles during
the twenty-one centuries that have elapsed since the death
of Alexander. The identification is confirmed by the fact
that the district in which Karâchi is situated is called K a r-
k a l l a to this day. Cunningham *Geog. of An. India*, I. p. 806.

a sandy island where they anchored and remained all next day. The country adjoining was
inhabited by an Indian race called the Arabies,
whom I have mentioned in my longer work, where
it is stated that they derive their name from the
River Arabis, which flows through their country
to the sea, and parts them from the Oreitai.[19]
Weighing from Krokala they had on their right
hand a mountain which the natives called Eiros,
and on their left a flat island almost level with
the sea, and so near the mainland to which it
runs parallel that the intervening channel is
extremely narrow. Having quite cleared this passage they come to anchor in a well-sheltered harbour, which Nearkhos, finding large and commodious, designated Alexander's Haven. This
harbour is protected by an island lying about 2
stadia off from its entrance. It is called Bibakta,
and all the country round about Sangada.[20] The
existence of the harbour is due altogether to the
island which opposes a barrier to the violence of
the sea. Here heavy gales blew from seaward for
many days without intermission, and Nearkhos

[19] The name of the Arabii is variously written,—Arabitæ,
Arbii, Arabies, Arbies, Aribes, Arbiti. The name of their
river has also several forms,—Arabis, Arabius, Artabis,
Artabius. It is now called the Puráli, the river which
flows through the present district of Las into the bay of
Sonmiyáni. The name of the Oreitai in Curtius is Horitæ.
Cunningham identifies them with the people on the Aghor
river, whom he says the Greeks would have named Agoritæ
or Aoritæ, by the suppression of the guttural, of which a
trace still remains in the initial aspirate of 'Horitæ.' Some
would connect the name with H a u r, a town which lay on
the route to Firabaz, in Mekrán.
[20] This name Sangada, D'Anville thought, survived in
that of a race of noted pirates who infested the shores of
the gulf of Kachh, called the S a n g a d i a n s or Sangarians.

w

fearing lest the barbarians might, some of them,
combine to attack and plunder the camp, fortified
his position with an enclosure of stones. Here
they were obliged to remain for 24 days. The
soldiers, we learn from Nearkhos, caught mussels
and oysters, and what is called the razor-fish,
these being all of an extraordinary size as compared
with the sorts found in our own sea.[21] He adds
that they had no water to drink but what was
brackish.

XXII. As soon as the monsoon ceased they
put again to sea, and having run fully 60 stadia
came to anchor at a sandy beach under shelter of
a desert island that lay near, called Domai.[22] On
the shore itself there was no water, but 20 stadia
inland it was procured of good quality. The following day they proceeded 300 stadia to Saranga,
where they did not arrive till night. They
anchored close to the shore, and found water at a
distance of about 8 stadia from it. Weighing from
Saranga they reach Sakala, a desert place, and
anchored. On leaving it they passed two rocks so
close to each other that the oar-blades of the
galleys grazed both, and after a course of 300
stadia they came to anchor at Morontobara.[23]

[21] "The pearl oyster abounds in 11 or 12 fathoms of
water all along the coast of Scinde. There was a fishery in
the harbour of Kurrachee which had been of some importance in the days of the native rulers."—*Wanderings of a
Naturalist in India*, p. 36.
[22] This island is not known, but it probably lay near the
rocky headland of Irus, now called M a n o r â, which protects the port of Karâchi from the sea and bad weather.
[23] "The name of Morontobara," says Cunningham, " I
would identify with Muâri, which is now applied to the
headland of Râs Muâri or Cape Monze, the last point of
the Pab range of mountains. *Bâra*, or *Bâri*, means a

The harbour here was deep and capacious, and well sheltered all round, and its waters quite tranquil, but the entrance into it was narrow. In the native language it was called Women's Haven, because a woman had been the first sovereign of the place. They thought it a great achievement to have passed those two rocks in safety, for when they were passing them the sea was boisterous and running high. They did not remain in Morontobara, but sailed the day after their arrival, when they had on their left hand an island which sheltered them from the sea, and which lay so near to the mainland that the intervening channel looked as if it had been artificially formed. Its length from one end to the other was 70 stadia.[24] The shore was woody and the island throughout over-grown with trees of every description. They were not able to get fairly through this passage

roadstead or haven; and Moranta is evidently connected with the Persian *Mard* a man, of which the feminine is still preserved in Káśmîrî as *Mahrin* a woman. From the distances given by Arrian, I am inclined to fix it at the mouth of the Bahar rivulet, a small stream which falls into the sea about midway between Cape Monze and Sonmiyâni." *Women's Haven* is mentioned by Ptolemy and Ammianus Marcellinus. There is in the neighbourhood a mountain now called M o r, which may be a remnant of the name Morontobari. The channel through which the fleet passed after leaving this place no longer exists, and the island has of course disappeared.

[24] The coast from Karâchi to the Purâli has undergone considerable changes, so that the position of the intermediate places cannot be precisely determined. "From Cape Monze to Sonmiyani," says Blair, "the coast bears evident marks of having suffered considerable alterations from the encroachments of the sea. We found trees which had been washed down, and which afforded us a supply of fuel. In some parts I saw imperfect creeks in a parallel direction with the coast. These might probably be the vestiges of that narrow channel through which the Greek galleys passed."

till towards daybreak, for the sea was not only rough, but also shoal, the tide being at ebb. They sailed on continuously, and after a course of 120 stadia anchored at the mouth of the river Arabis, where there was a spacious and very fine haven.[25] The water here was not fit for drinking, for the sea ran up the mouths of the Arabis. Having gone, however, about 40 stadia up the river, they found a pool from which, having drawn water, they returned to the fleet. Near the harbour is an island high and bare, but the sea around it supplied oysters and fish of various kinds.[26] As far as this, the country was possessed by the Arabies,

[25] Ptolemy and Marcian enumerate the following places as lying between the Indus and the Arabis: Rhizana, Koiamba, Women's Haven, Phagiaura, Arbis. Ptolemy does not mention the Oreitai, but extends the Arabii to the utmost limit of the district assigned to them in Arrian. He makes, notwithstanding the river Arabis to be the boundary of the Arabii. His Arabis must therefore be identified not with the *Pûrâli*, but with the *Kurmut*, called otherwise the *Rumra* or *Kalami*, where the position of Arrian's Kalama must be fixed. Pliny (vi. 25) places a people whom he calls the Arbii between the Oritae and Karmania, assigning as the boundary between the Arbii and the Oritae the river Arbis.

[26] The A r a b i s or P u r â l i discharges its waters into the bay of Sonmiyâni. "Sonmiyâni," says Kempthrone, "is a small town or fishing village situated at the mouth of a creek which runs up some distance inland. It is governed by a Sheikh, and the inhabitants appear to be very poor, chiefly subsisting on dried fish and rice. A very extensive bar or sandbank runs across the mouth of this inlet, and none but vessels of small burden can get over it even at high water, but inside the water is deep." The inhabitants of the present day are as badly off for water as their predecessors of old. "Everything," says one who visited the place, " is scarce, even water, which is procured by digging a hole five or six feet deep, and as many in diameter, in a place which was formerly a swamp; and if the water oozes, which sometimes it does not, it serves them that day, and perhaps the next, when it turns quite brackish, owing to the nitrous quality of the earth."

the last Indian people living in this direction;
and the parts beyond were occupied by the
Oreitai.[27]

XXIII. On weighing from the mouths of the
Arabis, they coasted the shores of the Oreitai, and
after running 200 stadia reached Pagala,[28] where
there was a surf but nevertheless good anchorage.
The crew were obliged to remain on board, a
party, however, being sent on shore to procure
water. They sailed next morning at sunrise, and
after a course of about 430 stadia, reached
Kabana[29] in the evening, where they anchored at
some distance from the shore, which was a desert;
the violence of the surf by which the vessels were
much tossed preventing them from landing.
While running the last course the fleet had been
caught in a heavy gale blowing from seaward,
when two galleys and a transport foundered.
All the men, however, saved themselves by swimming, as the vessels at the time of the disaster
were sailing close to the shore. They weighed

[27] Strabo agrees with Arrian in representing the Oreitai
as non-Indian. Cunningham, however, relying on statement made by Curtius, Diodorus and the Chinese pilgrim
Hwen Thsang, a most competent observer, considers them
to be of Indian origin, for their customs, according
to the Pilgrim, were like those of the people of Kachh, and
their written characters closely resembled those of India,
while their language was only slightly different. The
Oreitai as early as the 6th century B.C. were tributary
to Darius Hystaspes, and they were still subject to Persia
nearly 12 centuries later when visited by Hwen Thsang.—
Geog. of An. Ind. pp. 304 sqq.
[28] Another form is Pegadæ, met with in Philostratos,
who wrote a work on India.
[29] To judge from the distances given, this place should
be near the stream now called Agbor, on which is situated
Harkânâ. It is probably the Koiamba of Ptolemy.

from Kabana about midnight, and having proceeded 200 stadia arrived at Kôkala, where the
vessels *could not be drawn on shore,* but rode at
anchor out at sea. As the men, however, had
suffered severely by confinement on board,[30] and
were very much in want of rest, Nearkhos allowed
them to go on shore, where he formed a camp, forti-
fying it in the usual manner for protection against
the barbarians. In this part of the country Leonnatos, who had been commissioned by Alexander to
reduce the Oreitai and settle their affairs, defeated
that people and their allies in a great battle,
wherein all the leaders and 6,000 men were slain,
the loss of Leonnatos, being only 15 of his horse,
besides a few foot-soldiers, and *one man of note*
Apollophanês, the satrap of the Gedrosians.[31] A
full account, however, of these transactions is
given in my other work, where it is stated that for
this service Leonnatos had a golden crown placed
upon his head by Alexander in presence of the
Makedonian army. Agreeably to orders given
by Alexander, corn had been here collected for
the victualling of the vessels, and stores sufficient
to last for 10 days were put on board. Here
also such ships as had been damaged during the

---

[30] " In vessels like those of the Greeks, which afforded
neither space for motion, nor convenience for rest, the
continuing on board at night was always a calamity.
When a whole crew was to sleep on board, the suffering
was in proportion to the confinement."—Vincent, I.
p. 209 note.
[31] In another passage of Arrian (Anab. VI. 27, 1,) this
Apollophanês is said to have been deposed from his satrapy,
when Alexander was halting in the capital of Gedrôsia.
In the Journal Arrian follows Nearkhos, in the History,
Ptolemy or Aristobûlus.—Vincent.

voyage were repaired, while all the mariners that Nearkhos considered deficient in fortitude for the enterprise, he consigned to Leonnatos to be taken on by land, but at the same time he made good his complement of men by taking in exchange others more efficient from the troops under Leonnatos.

XXIV. From this place they bore away with a fresh breeze, and having made good a course of 500 stadia anchored near a winter torrent called the Tomêros, which at its mouth expanded into an estuary.[32] The natives lived on the marshy ground near the shore in cabins close and suffocating. Great was their astonishment when they descried the fleet approaching, but *they were not without courage*, and collecting in arms on the shore, drew up in line to attack the strangers when landing. They carried thick spears about 6 cubits long, not headed with iron, but what was as good, hardened at the point by fire. Their number was about 600, and when Nearkhos saw that they stood their ground prepared to fight, he ordered his vessels to advance, and then to anchor just within bowshot of the shore, for he had noticed that the thick spears of the barbarians were adapted only for close fight, and were by no means formidable as missiles. He then issued his directions: those men that were lightest equipped, and the most active and best at swim-

---

[32] From the distances given, the Tomêros must be identified with the M a k l o w or H i n g a l river; some would, however, make it the B h u s â l. The form of the name in Pliny is T o m b e r u s, and in Mela—T u b e r o. These authors mention another river in connection with the Tomêros,—the A r o s a p e s or A r u s a c e s.

ming were to swim to shore at a given signal:
when any one had swum so far that he could
stand in the water he was to wait for his next
neighbour, and not advance against the barbarians
until a file could be formed of three men deep:
that done, they were to rush forward shouting the
war-cry. The men selected for this service at once
plunged into the sea, and swimming rapidly touched
ground, still keeping due order, when forming in
file, they rushed to the charge, shouting the war-
cry, which was repeated from the ships, whence all
the while arrows and missiles from engines were
launched against the enemy. Then the barbarians
terrified by the glittering arms and the rapidity
of the landing, and wounded by the arrows and
other missiles, against which they had no protection, being all but entirely naked, fled at once
without making any attempt at resistance. Some
perished in the ensuing flight, others were taken
prisoners, and some escaped to the mountains.
Those they captured had shaggy hair, not only
on their head but all over their body; their nails
resembled the claws of wild beasts, and were used,
it would seem, instead of iron for dividing fish
and splitting the softer kinds of wood. Things
of a hard consistency they cut with sharp stones,
for iron they had none. As clothing they wore
the skins of wild beasts, and occasionally also the
thick skins of the large sorts of fish.[33]

XXV. After this action they draw the ships on

---

[33] Similar statements are made regarding this savage
race by Curtius IX. 10, 9; Diodôros XVII, 105; Pliny VI.
28; Strabo p. 720; Philostratos V.Ap. III., 57. Cf. Agatharkhides passim.—*Müller.*

shore and repair all that had been damaged. On
the 6th day they weighed again, and after a course
of 300 stadia reached a place called Malana, the
last on the coast of the Oreitai.[34] In the interior
these people dress like the Indians, and use
similar weapons, but differ from them in their
language and their customs. The length of the
coast of the Arabies, measured from the place
whence the expedition had sailed, was about 1,000
stadia, and the extent of the coast of the Oreitai
1,600 stadia. Nearkhos mentions that as they sailed
along the Indian coast (for the people beyond this
are not Indians), their shadows did not fall in the
usual direction, for when they stood out a good
way to the southward, their shadows appeared to
turn and fall southward.[35] Those constellations,

---

[34] Its modern representative is doubtless R â s M a l i n,
Malen or Moran.
[35] Such a phenomenon could not of course have
been observed at Malana, which is about 2 degrees
north of the Tropic, and Nearkhos, as has been already
noticed (Introd. p. 153), has on account mainly of this
statement been represented as a mendacious writer.
Schmieder and Gosselin attempt to vindicate him by
suggesting that Arrian in copying his journal had either
missed the meaning of this passage, or altered it to bring it
into accordance with his own geographical theories. Müller,
however, has a better and probably the correct explanation
to offer. He thinks that the text of Nearkhos which
Arrian used contained passages interpolated from Onêsikritos and writers of his stamp. The interpolations may
have been inserted by the Alexandrian geographers, who,
following Eratosthenes, believed that India lay between
the Tropics. In support of this view it is to be noted that
Arrian's account of the shadow occurs in that part of his
work where he is speaking of Malana of the Oreitai, and
that Pliny (VIII. 75) gives a similar account of the shadows
that fall on a mountain of a somewhat similar name in the
country of that very people. His words are: *In Indiae
gente Oretum Mons est Maleus nomine, juxta quem
umbrae aestate in Austrum, hieme in Septemtrionem*

x

moreover, which they had been accustomed to see
high in the heavens, were either not visible at all,
or were seen just on the verge of the horizon,
while the Polar constellations which had formerly been always visible now set and soon afterwards rose again. In this Nearkhos appears to
me to assert nothing improbable, for at Syênê in
Egypt they show a well in which, when the sun
is at the Tropic, there is no shadow at noon. In
Meroë also objects project no shadow at that
particular time. Hence it is probable that the
shadow is subject to the same law in India which
lies to the south, and more especially in the
Indian ocean, which extends still further to the
southward.

XXVI. Next to the Oreitai lies Gedrosia,[86] an
inland province through which Alexander led his
army, but this with difficulty, for the region was
so desolate that the troops in the whole course of
the expedition never suffered such direful extremities as on this march. But all the particulars

jaciuntur. Now Pliny was indebted for his knowledge of
Mons Maleus to Baeton, who places it however not in the
country of the Oreitai but somewhere in the lower Gangetic
region among the Suari and Monedes. It would thus
appear that what Baeton had said of *Mount Maleus* was
applied to *Malana* of the Oreitai, no doubt on account
of the likeness of the two names. Add to this that the
expression in the passage under consideration, *for the
people beyond this (Malana) are not Indians,* is no doubt
an interpolation into the text of the Journal, for it makes
the Oreitai to be an Indian people, whereas the Journal had
a little before made the Arabies to be the last people of
Indian descent living in this direction.

[86] This country, which corresponds generally to Mekrân, was called also Kedrosia, Gadrosia, or Gadrusia. The
people were an Arianian race akin to the Arakhosii, Arii,
and Drangiani.

relating to this I have set down in my larger
work (VI. 22-27). The seaboard below the Gedrosians is occupied by a people called the Ikhthyophagi, and along this country the fleet now pursued
its way. Weighing from Malana about the second
watch they ran a course of 600 stadia, and reached
Bagisâra. Here they found a commodious harbour,
and at a distance of 60 stadia from the sea a small
town called Pasira, whence the people of the neighbourhood were called Pasireës.[37] Weighing early
next morning they had to double a headland
which projected far out into the sea, and was high
and precipitous. Here having dug wells, and got
only a small supply of bad water, they rode at
anchor that day because a high surf prevented the
vessels approaching the shore. They left this
place next day, and sailed till they reached Kolta
after a course of 200 stadia.[38] Weighing thence at
daybreak they reached Kalama, after a course of

---

[37] Bagisara, says Kempthorne, "is now known by the
name of A r a b a h or H o r m a r a h Bay, and is deep and
commodious with good anchorage, sheltered from all winds
but those from the southward and eastward. The point
which forms this bay is very high and precipitous, and
runs out some distance into the sea. A rather large fishing
village is situated on a low sandy isthmus about one mile
across, which divides the bay from another. . . . . The
only articles of provision we could obtain from the inhabitants were a few fowls, some dried fish, and goats. They
grow no kind of vegetable or corn, a few water-melons
being the only thing these desolate regions bring forth.
Sandy deserts extend into the interior as far as the eye can
reach, and at the back of these rise high mountains." The
R h a p u a of Ptolemy corresponds to the Bagisara or
P a s i r a of Arrian, and evidently survives in the present
name of the bay and the headland of A r a b a.

[38] K o l t a.—A place unknown. It was situated on the
western side of the isthmus which connects R â s A r a b a
with the main land.

600 stadia, and there anchored.[39] Near the beach was a village around which grew a few palm-trees, the dates on which were still green. There was here an island called Karbinê, distant from the shore about 100 stadia.[40] The villagers by way

---

[39] A different form is Kaluboi. Situated on the river now called K a l a m i, or Kumra, or Kurmut, the Arabis of Ptolemy, who was probably misled by the likeness of the name to Karbis as the littoral district was designated here.

[40] Other forms—K a r n i n e, Karmina. The coast was probably called Karmin, if Karmis is represented in K u r m a t. The island lying twelve miles off the mouth of the Kalami is now called A s t o l a or S a n g a-d i p, which Kempthrone thus describes:—"Ashtola is a small desolate island about four or five miles in circumference, situated twelve miles from the coast of Mekrân. Its cliffs rise rather abruptly from the sea to the height of about 300 feet, and it is inaccessible except in one place, which is a sandy beach about one mile in extent on the northern side. Great quantities of turtle frequent this island for the purpose of depositing their eggs. Nearchus anchored off it, and called it Karnine. He says also that he received hospitable entertainment from its inhabitants, their presents being cattle and fish; but not a vestige of any habitation now remains. The Arabs come to this island, and kill immense numbers of these turtles,—not for the purpose of food, but they traffic with the shell to China, where it is made into a kind of paste, and then into combs, ornaments, &c., in imitation of tortoise-shell. The carcasses caused a stench almost unbearable. The only land animals we could see on the island were rats, and they were swarming. They feed chiefly on the dead turtle. The island was once famous as the rendezvous of the Jowassimee pirates." Vincent quotes Blair to this effect regarding the island :— "We were warned by the natives at Passence that it would be dangerous to approach the island of Asthola, as it was enchanted, and that a ship had been turned into a rock. The superstitious story did not deter us; we visited the island, found plenty of excellent turtle, and saw the rock alluded to, which at a distance had the appearance of a ship under sail. The story was probably told to prevent our disturbing the turtle. It has, however, some affinity to the tale of Nearchus's transport." As the enchanted island mentioned afterwards (chap. xxxi.), under the name of Nosala, was 100 stadia distant from the coast, it was probably the same as Karnine.

of showing their hospitality brought presents of
sheep and fish to Nearkhos, who says that the
mutton had a fishy taste like the flesh of sea birds
for the sheep fed on fish, there being no grass in
the place. Next day they proceeded 200 stadia,
and anchored off a shore near which lay a village
called Kissa, 30 stadia inland.[41] That coast was
however called Karbis. There they found little
boats such as might belong to miserably poor
fishermen, but the men themselves they saw
nothing of, for they had fled when they observed
the ships dropping anchor. No corn was here procurable, but a few goats had been left, which were
seized and put on board, for in the fleet provisions
now ran short. On weighing they doubled a
steep promontory, which projected about 150 stadia
into the sea, and then put into a well-sheltered
haven called Mosarna, where they anchored. Here
the natives were fishermen, and here they obtained
water.[42]

XXVII. From this place they took on board,
Nearkhos says, as pilot of the fleet, a Gedrosian
called Hydrakês, who undertook to conduct them
as far as Karmania.[43] Thenceforth until they

---

[41] Another form of the name is Kyss.
[42] The place according to Ptolemy is 900 stadia distant
from the Kalami river, but according to Marcianus 1,300
stadia. It must have been situated in the neighbourhood
of Cape Passence. The distances here are so great
exaggerated that the text is suspected to be corrupt or
disturbed. From Mosarna to Kophas the distance is
represented as 1,750 stadia, and yet the distance from Cape
Passence to Râs K o p p a (the Kophas of the text) is barely
500 stadia. According to Ptolemy and Marcian Karmania
begins at Mosarna, but according to Arrian much further
westward, at Badis near Cape Jask.
[43] " From the name given to this pilot I imagine that
he was an inhabitant of Hydriakus, a town near the bay

reached the Persian Gulf, the voyage was more practicable, and the names of the stations more familiar. Departing from Mosarna at night, they sailed 750 stadia, and reached the coast of Balômon. They touched next at Barna, which was 400 stadia distant.[44] Here grew many palm trees, and here was a garden wherein were myrtles and flowers from which the men wove chaplets for their hair.[45] They saw now for the first time cultivated trees, and met with natives in a condition above that of mere savages. Leaving this they followed the winding of the coast, and arrived at Dendrobosa, where they anchor in the open sea.[46] They weighed from this about midnight, and after a course of about 400 stadia gained the haven of

---

of Churber or Chewabad. . . . Upon the acquisition of Hydrakes or the Hydriakan two circumstances occur, that give a new face to the future course of the voyage, one is the very great addition to the length of each day's course ; and the other, that they generally weighed during the night : the former depending upon the confidence they acquired by having a pilot on board ; and the latter on the nature of the land breeze."—Vincent I., p. 244.

[44] This place is called in Ptolemy and Marcianus Badera or Bodera, and may have been situated near the Cape now called Chemaul Bunder. It is mentioned under the form Balara by Philostratos (Vit. Apoll. III. 56), whose description of the place is in close agreement with Arrian's.

[45] τῇσι κόμῃσιν. Another reading, not so good however, is, τῇσι κωμήτῃσιν for the village women, but the Greeks were not likely to have indulged in such gallantry. Wearing chaplets in the hair on festive occasions was a common practice with the Greeks. Cf. our author's Anab. V. 2. 8.

[46] In Ptolemy a place is mentioned called Derenoibila, which may be the same as this. The old name perhaps survives in the modern Daram or Duram, the name of a highland on part of the coast between Cape Passence and Cape Guadel.

Kôphas.[47] The inhabitants were fishermen possessed of small and wretched boats, which they
did not manage with oars fastened to a row-lock
according to the Grecian manner, but with paddles
which they thrust on this side, and on that into
the water, like diggers using a spade. They found
at this haven plenty of good water. Weighing
about the first watch they ran 800 stadia, and put
into Kyiza, where was a desert shore with a high
surf breaking upon it.[48] They were accordingly
obliged to let the ships ride at anchor and take
their meal on board. Leaving this they ran a
course of 500 stadia, and came to a small town
built on an eminence not far from the shore. On
turning his eyes in that direction Nearkhos
noticed that the land had some appearance of
being cultivated, and thereupon addressing
Arkhias (who was the son of Anaxidotos of Pella,
and sailed in the Commander's galley, being a
Makedonian of distinction) pointed out to him

[47] The name appears to survive in a cognominal Cape—
Râs Coppa. The natives use the same kind of boat to
this day; it is a curve made of several small planks nailed
or sewn together in a rude manner with cord made from
the bark of date trees and called *kair*, the whole being
then smeared over with dammer or pitch.—*Kempthorne.*

[48] According to Ptolemy and Marcianus this place lay
400 stadia to the west of the promontory of Alambator (now
Râs Guadel). Some trace of the word may be recognized
in R â s G h u n s e, which now designates a point of land
situated about those parts. Arrian passes Cape Guadel
without notice. "We should be reasonably surprised at
this," says Vincent (I. 248), "as the doubling of a cape is
always an achievement in the estimation of a Greek navigator; but having now a native pilot on board, it is evident
he took advantage of the land-breeze to give the fleet an
offing. This is clearly the reason why we hear nothing in
Arrian of Ptolemy's Alabagium, or Alambateir, the prominent feature of this coast."

that they must take possession of the place, as the inhabitants would not willingly supply the army with food. It could not however be taken by assault, a tedious siege would be necessary, and they were already short of provisions. But the country was one that produced corn as the thick stubble which they saw covering the fields near the shore clearly proved. This proposal being approved of by all, he ordered Arkhias to make a feint of preparing the fleet, all but one ship to sail, while he himself, pretending to be left behind with that ship, approached the town as if merely to view it.

XXVIII. When he approached the walls the inhabitants came out to meet him, bringing a present of tunny-fish broiled in pans (the first instance of cookery among the Ikhthyophagi, although these were the very last of them), accompanied with small cakes and dates. He accepted their offering with the proper acknowledgments, but said he wished to see their town, which he was accordingly allowed to enter. No sooner was he within the gates than he ordered two of his archers to seize the portal by which they had entered, while he himself with two attendants and his interpreter mounting the wall hard by, made the preconcerted signal, on seeing which the troops under Arkhias were to perform the service assigned to them. The Makedonians, on seeing the signal, immediately ran their ships towards land, and without loss of time jumped into the sea. The barbarians, alarmed at these proceedings, flew to arms. Upon this Nearkhos ordered his interpreter to proclaim that if they wished their city to be preserved from pillage they must supply his army

193

with provisions. They replied that they had none, and proceeded to attack the wall, but were repulsed by the archers with Nearkhos, who assailed them with arrows from the summit of the wall. Accordingly, when they saw that their city was taken, and on the point of being pillaged, they at once begged Nearkhos to take whatever corn they had, and to depart without destroying the place. Nearkhos upon this orders Arkhias to possess himself of the gates and the ramparts adjoining, and sends at the same time officers to see what stores were available, and whether these would be all honestly given up. The stores were produced, consisting of a kind of meal made from fish roasted, and a little wheat and barley, for the chief diet of these people was fish with bread added as a relish. The troops having appropriated these supplies returned to the fleet, which then hauled off to a cape *in the neighbourhood* called Bagia, which the natives regarded as sacred to the sun.[49]

XXIX. They weighed from this cape about midnight, and having made good a course of 1,000 stadia, put into Talmena, where they found a harbour with good anchorage.[50] They sailed

[49] *The little town attacked by Nearchus* lay on Gwattar Bay. The promontory in its neighbourhood called B a g i a is mentioned by Ptolemy and Marcianus, the latter of whom gives its distance from Kyiza at 250 stadia, which is but half the distance as given by Arrian. To the west of this was the river Kaudryaces or Hydriaces, the modern Baghwar Dasti or Muhani river, which falls into the Bay of Gwattar.
[50] A name not found elsewhere. To judge by the distance assigned, it must be placed on what is now called Chaubar Bay, on the shores of which are three towns, one being called T i z,—perhaps the modern representative of Tisa, a place in those parts mentioned by Ptolemy, and which may have been the Talmena of Arrian.

y

thence to Kanasis, a deserted town 400 stadia distant, where they find a well ready-dug and wild palm-trees.[51] These they cut down, using the tender heads to support life since provisions had again run scarce. They sailed all day and all night suffering great distress from hunger, and then came to an anchor off a desolate coast. Nearkhos fearing lest the men, if they landed, would in despair desert the fleet, ordered the ships to be moved to a distance from shore. Weighing from this they ran a course of 850 stadia, and came to anchor at Kanate, a place with an open beach and some water-courses.[52] Weighing again, and making 800 stadia, they reach Taoi, where they drop anchor.[53] The place contained some small and wretched villages, which were deserted by the inhabitants upon the approach of the fleet. Here the men found a little food and dates of the palm-tree, beside seven camels left by the villagers which were killed for food. Weighing thence about daybreak they ran a course of 300 stadia, and came to anchor at Dagasira, where the people were nomadic.[54] Weighing again they sailed all night and all day without intermission, and having thus accomplished a course of 1,100

---

[51] The name is not found elsewhere. It must have been situated on a bay enclosed within the two headlands Râs Fuggem and Râs Godem.

[52] Kanate probably stood on the site of the modern Kungoun, which is near Râs Kalat, and not far from the river Bunth.

[53] Another and the common form is Troisi. The villages of the Taoi must have been where the Sudich river enters the sea. Here Ptolemy places his Kommana or Nommana and his follower Marcian his Ommana. See ante p. 104 note.

[54] The place in Ptolemy is called Agrispolis,—in Marcianus, Agrisa. The modern name is Girishk.

stadia, left behind them the nation of the Ikhthyophagi, on whose shores they had suffered such
severe privations. They could not approach the
beach on account of the heavy surf, but rode at
anchor out at sea. In navigating the Ikhthyophagi
coast the distance traversed was not much short
of 10,000 stadia. The people, as their name
imports, live upon fish. Few of them, however, are
fishermen, and what fish they obtain they owe
mostly to the tide at whose reflux they catch them
with nets made for this purpose. These nets are
generally about 2 stadia long, and are composed
of the bark (or fibres) of the palm, which they
twine into cord in the same way as the fibres of
flax are twined. When the sea recedes, hardly any
fish are found among the dry sands, but they
abound in the depressions of the surface where the
water still remains. The fish are for the most part
small, though some are caught of a considerable size,
these being taken in the nets. The more delicate
kinds they eat raw as soon as they are taken out of
the water. The large and coarser kinds they dry in
the sun, and when properly dried grind into a sort
of meal from which they make bread. This meal is
sometimes also used to bake cakes with. The cattle
as well as their masters fare on dried fish, for the
country has no pastures, and hardly even a blade of
grass. In most parts crabs, oysters and mussels add
to the means of subsistence. Natural salt is found
in the country, * * * from these they make oil.[56]

---

[56] Schmieder suggests that instead of the common
reading here ἀπὸ τούτων ἔλαιον ποιέουσιν Arrian may
have written ἀπὸ θύννων ε. π. *they make oil from thun-
nies,* i. e. use the fat for oil.

Certain of their communities inhabit deserts where
not a tree grows, and where there are not even
wild fruits. Fish is their sole means of subsistence. In some few places, however, they sow
with grain some patches of land, and eat the
produce as a viand of luxury along with the fish
which forms the staple of their diet. The better
class of the population in building their houses
use, instead of wood, the bones of whales stranded
on the coast, the broadest bones being employed
in the framework of the doors. Poor people, and
those are the great majority, construct their
dwellings with the backbones of fish.[56]

XXX. Whales of enormous size frequent the
outer ocean, besides other fish larger than those
found in the Mediterranean. Nearkhos relates that
when they were bearing away from Kyiza, the
sea early in the morning was observed to be blown
up into the air as if by the force of a whirlwind.
The men greatly alarmed enquired of the pilots
the nature and cause of this phenomenon, and
were informed that it proceeded from the blowing
of the whales as they sported in the sea. This
report did not quiet their alarm, and through
astonishment they let the oars drop from their
hands. Nearkhos, however, recalled them to duty,
and encouraged them by his presence, ordering
the prows of those vessels that were near him to
be turned as in a sea-fight towards the creatures
as they approached, while the rowers were just
then to shout as loud as they could the *alala,*

---

[56] "This description of the natives, with that of their
mode of living and the country they inhabit, is strictly
correct even to the present day."—Kempthorne.

and swell the noise by dashing the water rapidly
with the oars. The men thus encouraged on
seeing the preconcerted signal advanced to action.
Then, as they approached the monsters, they
shouted the *alala* as loud as they could bawl, sound-
ed the trumpets, and ‘dashed the water noisily
with the oars. Thereupon the whales, which were
seen ahead, plunged down terror-struck into the
depths, and soon after rose astern, when they
vigorously continued their blowing. The men
by loud acclamations expressed their joy at this
unexpected deliverance, the credit of which they
gave to Nearkhos, who had shown such admirable
fortitude and judgment.

We learn further, that on many parts of the coast
whales are occasionally stranded, being left in
shallow water at ebb-tide, and thus prevented
from escaping back to sea, and that they are
sometimes also cast ashore by violent storms.
Thus perishing, their flesh rots away, and gradually drops off till the bones are left bare. These
are used by the natives in the construction of their
huts, the larger ribs making suitable bearing
beams, and the smaller serving for rafters. The
jaw-bones make arches for the door-ways, for
whales are sometimes five and twenty *orguiœ*
(fathoms) in length.[57]

XXXI. When they were sailing along the
Ikhthyophagi coast, they were told about an
island which was said to be about 100 stadia dis-

---

[57] Strabo (XV. ii. 12, 13) has extracted from Nearkhos
the same passage regarding whales. See Nearchi fragm.
25. Cf Onesikritos (fr. 30) and Orthagoras in Aelian. N. An.
XVII. 6; Diodor. XVII, 106; Curtius X. 1, 11.

tant from the mainland, and uninhabited. Its name was Nosala, and it was according to the local tradition sacred to the sun. No one willingly visited this island, and if any one was carried to it unawares, he was never more seen. Nearkhos states that a transport of his fleet, manned with an Egyptian crew, disappeared not far from this island, and that the pilots accounted for their disappearance by saying that they must have landed on the island in ignorance of the danger which they would thereby incur. Nearkhos, however, sent a galley of 30 oars to sail round the island, instructing the men not to land, but to approach as near as they could to the shore, and hail the men, shouting out the name of the captain or any other name they had not forgotten. No one answered to the call, and Nearkhos says that he then sailed in person to the island, and compelled his company much against their will to go on shore. He too landed, and showed that the story about the island was nothing but an empty fable. Concerning this same island he heard also another story, which ran to this effect: it had been at one time the residence of one of the Nereids, whose name, he says, he could not learn. It was her wont to have intercourse with any man who visited the island, changing him thereafter into a fish, and casting him into the sea. The sun, however, being displeased with the Nereid, ordered her to remove from the island. She agreed to do this, and seek a home elsewhere, but stipulated that she should be cured of her malady. To this condition the sun assented, and then the Nereid, taking pity upon

the men whom she had transformed into fish,
restored them to their human shape. These men
were the progenitors of the Ikhthyophagi, the
line of succession remaining unbroken down to
the time of Alexander. Now, for my part I have
no praise to bestow on Nearkhos for expending
so much time and ingenuity on the not very
difficult task of proving the falsehood of these
stories, for, to take up antiquated fables merely
with a view to prove their falsehood, I can only
regard as a contemptible piece of folly.[58]

XXXII. To the Ikhthyophagi succeed the
Gadrôsii, who occupy a most wretched tract of
country full of sandy deserts, in penetrating
which Alexander and his army were reduced to
the greatest extremities, of which an account is to
be found in my other work. But this is an inland region, and therefore when the expedition
left the Ikhthyophagi, its course lay along Karmania.[59] Here, when they first drew towards shore,

[58] The story of the Nereid is evidently an Eastern
version of the story of the enchantress Kirkê. The island
here called Nosala is that already mentioned under the
name of Karbine, now Astbola.

[59] Karmania extended from Cape Jask to Râs
Nabend, and comprehended the districts now called
Moghostân, Kirman, and Lâristan. Its metropolis, according to Ptolemy, was Karmana, now Kirman, which
gives its name to the whole province. The first port in
Karmania reached by the expedition was in the neighbourhood of Cape Jask, where the coast is described as being
very rocky, and dangerous to mariners on account of shoals
and rocks under water. Kempthorne says: "The cliffs
along this part of the coast are very high, and in many
places almost perpendicular. Some have a singular appearance, one near Jask being exactly of the shape of a quoin
or wedge; and another is a very remarkable peak, being
formed by three stones, as if placed by human hands,
one on the top of the other. It is very high, and has the
resemblance of a chimney."

they could not effect a landing, but had to remain
all night on board anchored in the deep, because
a violent surf spread along the shore and far out
to sea. Thereafter the direction of their course
changed, and they sailed no longer towards sunset,
but turned the heads of the vessels more to
the north-west. Karmania is better wooded and
produces better fruit than the country either
of the Ikhthyophagi or the Oreitai. It is also
more grassy, and better supplied with water.
They anchor next at Badis, an inhabited place in
Karmania, where grew cultivated trees of many
different kinds, with the exception of the olive, and
where also the soil favoured the growth of the
vine and of corn.[60] Weighing thence they ran
800 stadia, and came to an anchor off a barren
coast, whence they descried a headland projecting
far out into the sea, its nearest extremity being to
appearance about a day's sail distant. Persons
acquainted with those regions asserted that this
cape belonged to Arabia, and was called Maketa,
whence cinnamon and other products were exported
to the Assyrians.[61] And from this coast where

---

[60] Badis must have been near where the village of Jask
now stands, beyond which was the promontory now called
Râs Kerazi or Keroot or Bombarak, which marks the
entrance to the Straits of Ormus. This projection is the
Cape Karpella of Ptolemy. Badis may be the same as the
Kanthatis of this geographer.

[61] Maketa is now called Cape Mesandum in Omân. It is
thus described by Palgrave in the Narrative of his Travels
through Central and Eastern Arabia (Vol. II. pp. 316-7).
The afternoon was already far advanced when we reached
the headland, and saw before us the narrow sea-pass which
runs between the farthest rocks of Mesandum and the
mainland of the Cape. This strait is called the " Bab" or
" gate :" it presents an imposing spectacle, with lofty pre-
cipices on either side, and the water flowing deep and black

the fleet was now anchored, and from the headland which they saw projecting into the sea right opposite, the gulf in my opinion (which is also that of Nearkhos) extends up into the interior, and is probably the Red Sea. When this headland was now in view Onesikritos, *the chief pilot*, proposed that they should proceed to explore it, and by so shaping their course, escape the distressing passage up the gulf; but Nearkhos opposed this proposal. Onesikritos, he said, must be wanting in ordinary judgment if he did not know with what design Alexander had sent the fleet on this voyage. He certainly had not sent it, because there were no proper means of conducting the whole army safely by land, but his express purpose was to obtain a knowledge of the coasts they might pass on their voyage, together with the harbours and islets, and to have the bays that might occur explored, and to ascertain whether there were towns bordering on the ocean, and whether the countries were habitable or desert. They ought not therefore to lose sight of this object, seeing that they were now near the end of their toils, and especially that they were no longer in want of the necessary supplies for prosecuting the voyage.

---

below; the cliffs are utterly bare and extremely well adapted for shivering whatever vessels have the ill luck to come upon them. Hence and from the ceaseless dash of the dark waves, the name of "Mosandum" or "Anvil," a term seldom better applied. But this is not all, for some way out at sea rises a huge square mass of basalt of a hundred feet and more in height sheer above the water; it bears the name of "Salâmah" or "safety," a euphemism of good augury for "danger." Several small jagged peaks, just projecting above the surface, cluster in its neighbourhood; these bear the endearing name of "Benât Salâmah," or "Daughters of Salâmah."

z

He feared, moreover, since the headland stretched
towards the south, lest they should find the
country there a parched desert destitute of water
and insufferably hot. This argument prevailed,
and it appears to me that by this counsel Nearkhos
saved the expedition, for all accounts represent
this cape and the parts adjacent as an arid waste
where water cannot possibly be procured.

XXXIII. On resuming the voyage they sailed
close to land, and after making about 700 stadia
anchored on another shore called Neoptana.[62]
From this they weighed next day at dawn, and
after a course of 100 stadia anchored at the mouth
of the river Anamis[63] in a country called Harmozeia.[64] Here at last they found a hospitable

---

[62] This place is not mentioned elsewhere, but must have
been situated somewhere, in the neighbourhood of the
village of Karun.

[63] The Anamis, called by Pliny the Ananis, and by
Ptolemy and Mela the Andanis, is now the Minâb or Ibrahim River.

[64] Other forms—Hormazia, Armizia regio. The name
was transferred from the mainland to the island now called
Ormus, when the inhabitants fled thither to escape from
the Moghals. It is called by Arrian Organa (chap.
xxxvii.) The Arabians called it Djerun, a name which it
continued to bear up to the 12th century. Pliny mentions
an island called Oguris, of which perhaps Djerun is a
corruption. He ascribes to it the honour of having been
the birthplace of Erythres. The description, however,
which he gives of it is more applicable to the island called
by Arrian (chap. xxxvii.) Oârakta (now Kishm) than to
Ormus. Arrian's description of Harmozia is still applicable
to the region adjacent to the Minâb. "It is termed," says
Kempthorne, "the Paradise of Persia. It is certainly most
beautifully fertile, and abounds in orange groves, orchards
containing apples, pears, peaches, and apricots, with vine-
yards producing a delicious grape, from which was made
at one time a wine called Amber rosolia, generally considered the white wine of Kishma; but no wine is made here
now." The old name of Kishma—Oârakta—is preserved
in one of its modern names, Vrokt or Brokt.

region, one which was rich in every production
except only the olive. Here accordingly they
landed, and enjoyed a welcome respite from their
many toils—heightening their pleasure by calling
to remembrance what miseries they had suffered
at sea and in the Ikhthyophagi country, where
the shores were so sterile, and the natives so
brute-like, and where they had been reduced to
the last extremities of want. Here, also, some of
them in scattered parties, leaving the encampment on the shore, wandered inland searching for
one thing and another that might supply their
several requirements. While thus engaged, they
fell in with a man who wore a Greek mantle,
and was otherwise attired as a Greek and spoke
the Greek language. Those who first discovered
him declared that tears started to their eyes, so
strange did it appear, after all they had suffered,
to see once more a countryman of their own, and
to hear the accents of their native tongue. They
asked him whence he came, and who he was.
He replied that he had straggled from the army of
Alexander, and that the army led by Alexander in
person was not far off. On hearing this they hurry
the man with shouts of tumultuous joy to the presence of Nearkhos, to whom he repeated all that he
had already said, assuring him that the army
and the king were not more than a 5 days' march
distant from the sea. The Governor of the province, he added, was on the spot, and he would
present him to Nearkhos, and he presented him
accordingly. Nearkhos consulted this person regarding the route he should take in order to
reach the king, and then they all went off, and made

their way to the ships. Early next morning the
ships by orders of Nearkhos were drawn on shore,
partly for repair of the damages which some of
them had suffered on the voyage, and partly
because he had resolved to leave here the greater
part of his army. Having this in view, he fortified
the roadstead with a double palisade, and also
with an earthen rampart and a deep ditch extending from the banks of the river to the dockyard
where the ships were lying.

XXXIV. While Nearkhos was thus occupied,
the Governor being aware that Alexander was in
great anxiety about the fate of this expedition,
concluded that he would receive some great advantage from Alexander should he be the first to
apprize him of the safety of the fleet and of the
approaching visit of Nearkhos. Accordingly he
hastened to Alexander by the shortest route, and
announced that Nearkhos was coming from the
fleet to visit him. Alexander, though he could
scarcely believe the report, nevertheless received
the tidings with all the joy that might have been
expected.

Day after day, however, passed without confirma-
tion of the fact, till Alexander, on comparing the
distance from the sea with the date on which the
report had reached him, at last gave up all belief
in its truth, the more especially as several of the
parties which he had successively despatched to
find Nearkhos and escort him to the camp, had
returned without him, after going a short distance,
and meeting no one, while others who had prose-
cuted the search further, and failed to find Nearkhos
and his company were still absent. He therefore

ordered the Governor into confinement for having
brought delusive intelligence and rendered his
vexation more acute by the disappointment of his
hopes, and indeed his looks and perturbation of
mind plainly indicated that he was pierced to the
heart with a great grief. Meanwhile, however, one
of the parties that had been despatched in search
of Nearkhos, and his escort being furnished with
horses and waggons for their accommodation, fell
in on the way with Nearkhos and Arkhias, who
were followed by five or six attendants. At first
sight they recognized neither the admiral himself
nor Arkhias, so much changed was their appearance, their hair long and neglected, their persons
filthy, encrusted all over with brine and shrivelled,
their complexion sallow from want of sleep and
other severe privations. On their asking where
Alexander was, they were told the name of the
place. Arkhias then, perceiving who they were,
said to Nearkhos—"It strikes me, Nearkhos, these
men are traversing the desert by the route we
pursue, for no other reason than because they have
been sent to our relief. True, they did not know us,
but that is not at all surprising, for our appearance
is so wretched that we are past all recognition.
Let us tell them who we are, and ask them why they
are travelling this way." Nearkhos, thinking he
spoke with reason, asked the men whither they were
bound. They replied that they were searching for
Nearkhos and the fleet. "Well! I am Nearkhos,"
said the admiral, "and this man here is Arkhias.
Take us under your conduct, and we will report to
Alexander the whole history of the expedition."

XXXV. They were accordingly accommodated

in the waggons, and conducted to the camp. Some
of the horsemen, however, wishing to be the first
to impart the news, hastened forward, and told
Alexander that Nearkhos himself, and Arkhias
with him, and five attendants, would soon arrive,
but to enquiries about the rest of the people in
the expedition they had no information to give.
Alexander, concluding from this that all the expedition had perished except this small band,
which had been unaccountably saved, did not so
much feel pleasure for the preservation of Nearkhos and Arkhias as distress for the loss of his
whole fleet. During this conversation Nearkhos
and Arkhias arrived. It was not without difficulty Alexander after a close scrutiny recognized
who the hirsute, ill-clad men who stood before
him were, and being confirmed by their misera-
able appearance in his belief that the expedition
had perished, he was still more overcome with
grief. At length he held out his hand to Nearkhos, and leading him apart from his attendants
and his guards he burst into tears, and wept for a
long time. Having, after a good while, recovered
some composure, "Nearkhos!" he says, "since you
and Arkhias have been restored to me alive, I can
bear more patiently the calamity of losing all my
fleet; but tell me now, in what manner did the
vessels and my people perish." "O my king!" replied Nearkhos, "the ships are safe and the people
also, and we are here to give you an account of their
preservation." Tears now fell much faster from
his eyes than before, but they were tears of joy for
the salvation of his fleet which he had given up for
lost. "And where are now my ships," he then

enquired. " They are drawn up on shore," replied Nearkhos, " on the beach of the river Anamis for repairs." Upon this Alexander, swearing by Zeus of the Greeks and Ammon of the Libyans, declared that he felt happier at receiving these tidings than in being the conqueror of all Asia, for, had the expedition been lost, the blow to his peace of mind would have been a counterpoise to all the success he had achieved.

XXXVI. But the Governor whom Alexander had put into confinement for bringing intelligence that appeared to be false, seeing Nearkhos in the camp, sunk on his knees before him, and said: " I am the man who brought to Alexander the news of your safe arrival. You see how I am situated." Nearkhos interceded with Alexander on his behalf, and he was then liberated. Alexander next proceeded to offer a solemn sacrifice in gratitude for the preservation of his fleet unto Zeus the Preserver, and Heraklês, and Apollo the Averter of Destruction, and unto Poseidôn, and every other deity of ocean. He celebrated likewise a contest in gymnastics and music, and exhibited a splendid procession wherein a foremost place was assigned to Nearkhos. Chaplets were wreathed for his head, and flowers were showered upon him by the admiring multitude. At the end of these proceedings the king said to Nearkhos, " I do not wish you, Nearkhos, either to risk your life or expose yourself again to the hardships of sea-voyaging, and I shall therefore send some other officer to conduct the expedition onward to Sousa." But Nearkhos answered, and said : " It is my duty, O king ! as it is also my

desire, in all things to obey you, but if your object
is to gratify me in some way, do not take the
command from me until I complete the voyage
by bringing the ships in safety to Sousa. I have
been trusted to execute that part of the undertaking in which all its difficulty and danger lay;
transfer not, then, to another the remaining part,
which hardly requires an effort, and that, too, just
at the time when the glory of final success is
ready to be won." Alexander scarcely allowed
him to conclude his request, which he granted
with grateful acknowledgment of his services.[65]
Then he sent him down again to the coast
with only a small escort, believing that the
country through which he would pass was
friendly. He was not permitted however to
pursue his way to the coast without opposition,
for the barbarians, resenting the action of
Alexander in deposing their satrap, had gathered
in full force and seized all the strongholds
of Karmania before Tlepolemos, the newly appointed Governor, had yet succeeded in fully
establishing his authority.[66] It happened therefore that several times in the course of a day
Nearkhos encountered bands of the insurgents
with whom he had to do battle. He therefore hurried forward without lingering by the
way, and reached the coast in safety, though
not without severe toil and difficulty. On arriv-

[65] Diodôros (XVII. 106) gives quite a different account of
the visit of Nearkhos to Alexander.
[66] The preceding satrap was Sibyrtios, the friend of
Megasthenês. He had been transferred to govern the
Gadrosians and the Arakhotians.

ing he sacrificed to Zeus the Preserver, and celebrated gymnastic games.

XXXVII. These pious rites having been duly performed, they again put to sea, and, after passing a desolate and rocky island, arrived at another island, where they ânchored. This was one of considerable size and inhabited, and 300 stadia distant from Harmozeia, the harbour which they had last left. The desert island was called Organa, and that where they anchored Oärakta.[67] It produced vines, palm-trees, and corn. Its length is 800 stadia. Mazênês, the chief of this island, accompanied them all the way to Sousa, having volunteered to act as pilot of the fleet. The natives of the island professed to point out the tomb of the very first sovereign of the country, whose name they said was Erythrês, after whom the sea in that part of the world was called the Erythraean.[68] Weighing thence their course lay

[67] As stated in Note 64, Organa is now *Ormuz*, and Oarakta, *Kishm*. Ormuz, once so renowned for its wealth and commerce, that it was said of it by its Portuguese occupants, that if the world were a golden ring, Ormuz would be the diamond signet, is now in utter decay. "I have seen," says Palgrave (II. 319), the abasement of Tyre, the decline of Surat, the degradation of Goa : but in none of those fallen seaports is aught resembling the utter desolation of Ormuz." A recent traveller in Persia (Binning) thus describes the coast : "It presents no view but sterile, barren, and desolate chains of rocks and hills : and the general aspect of the Gulf is dismal and forbidding. Moore's charming allusions to Oman's sea, with its ' banks of pearl and palmy isles' are unfortunately quite visionary ; for uglier and more unpicturesque scenery I never beheld." —*Two Years' Travel in Persia*, I. pp. 136, 137.
[68] For the legend of Erythres see Agatharkhides De Mari Eryth. I. 1-4 and Strabo XVI. iv. 20. The Erythraean Sea included the Indian Ocean, the Persian Gulf, and the Red Sea, the last being called also the Arabian Gulf, when it was necessary to distinguish it from the Erythraean

along the island, and they anchored on its shores
at a place whence another island was visible at a
distance of about 40 stadia. They learned that it
was sacred to Poseidôn, and inaccessible.[69] Next
morning, as they were putting out to sea, the ebb-
tide caught them with such violence that three of
the galleys were stranded on the beach, and the rest
of the fleet escaped with difficulty from the surf
into deep water. The stranded vessels were however floated off at the return of the tide, and the
day after rejoined the fleet. They anchored at
another island distant from the mainland somewhere about 300 stadia, after running a course
of 400 stadia. Towards daybreak they resumed
the voyage, passing a desert island which lay on

Taub

---

in general. It can hardly be doubted that the epithet
Erythræan (which means *red*, Greek ἐρυθρὸς) first
designated the Arabian Gulf or Red Sea, and was afterwards
extended to the seas beyond the Straits by those who first
explored them. The Red Sea was so called because it
washed the shores of Arabia, called *the Red Land* (Edom),
in contradistinction to Egypt, called *the Black Land*
(Kemi), from the darkness of the soil deposited by the
Nile. Some however thought that it received its name
from the quantity of red coral found in its waters, especially along the eastern shores, and Strabo says (loc. cit.):
"Some say that the sea is red from the colour arising from
reflexion either from the sun, which is vertical, or from
the mountains, which are red by being scorched with
intense heat; for the colour it is supposed may be produced
by both of these causes. Ktesias of Knidos speaks of a
spring which discharges into the sea a red and ochrous
water."—Cf. Eustath. Comment. 38.

[69] This island is that now called A n g a r, or H a n j a m,
to the south of Kishm. It is described as being nearly
destitute of vegetation and uninhabited. Its hills, of
volcanic origin, rise to a height of 300 feet. The other
island, distant from the mainland about 300 stadia, is now
called the Great Tombo, near which is a smaller island
called Little Tombo. They are low, flat, and uninhabited.
They are 25 miles distant from the western extremity of
Kishm.

their left, called Pylôra, and anchored at Sisidônê, a small town which could supply nothing but water and fish.[70] Here again the natives were fish eaters, for the soil was utterly sterile. Having taken water on board, they weighed again, and having run 300 stadia, anchored at Tarsia, the extremity of a cape which projects far into the sea. The next place of anchorage was Kataia, a desert island, and very flat.[71] It was said to be sacred to Hermês and Aphroditê. The length of this course was 300 stadia. To this island sheep and goats are annually sent by the people of the adjoining continent who consecrate them to Hermês and Aphroditê. These animals were to be seen running about in a wild state, the effect of time and the barren soil.

XXXVIII. Karmania extends as far as this island, but the parts beyond appertain to Persia. The extent of the Karmanian coast was 3,700

isles belong to Karmania

---

[70] The island of Pylora is that now called Polior. Sisidone appears in other forms—Prosidodone, proSidodone, pros Sidone, pros Dodone. Kempthorne thought this was the small fishing village- now called Mogos, situated in a bay of the same name. The name may perhaps be preserved in the name of a village in the same neighbourhood, called Dnan Tarsia—now Râs-el-Djard —described as high and rugged, and of a reddish colour.

[71] Kataia is now the island called Kaes or Kenn. Its character has altered, being now covered with dwarf trees, and growing wheat and tobacco. It supplies ships with refreshment, chiefly goats and sheep and a few vegetables. "At morning," says Binning (I.137), "we passed Polior, and at noon were running along the South side of the Isle of Keesh, called in our maps Kenn; a fertile and populous island about 7 miles in length. The inhabitants of this, as well as of every other island in the Gulf, are of Arab blood—for every true Persian appears to hate the very sight of the sea."

stadia.[72] The people of this province live like the
Persians. on whom they border, and they have
similar weapons and a similar military system.
When the fleet left the sacred island, its course lay
along the coast of Persis, and it first drew to land
at a place called Ila, where there is a harbour under
cover of a small and desert island called Kaï-
kander.[73] The distance run was 400 stadia.
Towards daybreak they came to another island
which was inhabited, and anchored thereon. Nearkhos notices that there is here a fishery for
pearl as there is in the Indian Sea.[74] Having
sailed along the shores of the promontory in
which this island terminates, a distance of about
40 stadia, they came to an anchor upon its
shores. The next anchorage was in the vicinity
of a lofty hill called Okhos, where the harbour
was well sheltered and the inhabitants were
fishermen.[75] Weighing thence they ran a course of

[72] The boundary between Karmania and Persis was
formed by a range of mountains opposite the island of
K a t a i a. Ptolemy, however, makes Karmania extend
much further, to the river B a g r a d a s, now called the
N a b a n or N a b e n d.

[73] K a i k a n d e r has the other forms—Kekander, Ki-
kander, Kaskandrus, Karkundrus, Karskandrus, Sasækan-
der. This island, which is now called I n d e r a b i a, or
A n d a r a v i a, is about four or five miles from the mainland,
having a small town on the north side, where is a safe and
commodious harbour. The other island mentioned immediately after is probably that now called Busheab. It is,
according to Kempthorne, a low, flat island, about eleven
miles from the mainland, containing a small town principally inhabited by Arabs, who live on fish and dates.
The harbour has good anchorage even for large vessels.

[74] The pearl oyster is found from Ras Musendom to the
head of the Gulf. There are no famed banks on the Persian
side, but near Bushire there are some good ones.

[75] A p o s t a n a was near a place now called S c h e v a r.
It is thought that the name may be traced in D a h r a

400 stadia, which brought them to Apostana, where they anchored. At this station they saw a great many boats, and learned that at a distance of 60 stadia from the shore there was a village. From Apostana they weighed at night, and proceeded 400 stadia to a bay, on the borders of which many villages were to be seen. Here the fleet anchored under the projection of a cape which rose to a considerable height.[76] Palm-trees and other fruit-bearing trees similar to those of Greece, adorned the country round. On weighing thence they sailed in a line with the coast, and after a course of somewhere about 600 stadia reached Gôgana, which was an inhabited place, where they anchored at the mouth of a winter torrent called the Areôn. It was difficult to anchor, for the approach to the mouth of the river was by a narrow channel, since the ebbing of the tide had left shoals which lay all round in a circle.[77] Weighing thence they gained, after running as many as 800 stadia, the mouth of another river called the Sitakos, where also it was troublesome to anchor. Indeed all along the coast of Persis the fleet had to be navigated through shoals and breakers and oozy channels.

Ahbân, an adjacent mountain ridge of which Okhos was probably the southern extremity.

[76] This bay is that on which Naban or Nabend is now situated. It is not far from the river called by Ptolemy the Bagradas. The place abounds with palm-trees as of old.

[77] Gôgana is now Konkan or Konaun. The bay lacks depth of water; a stream still falls into it—the Areon of the text. To the north-west of this place in the interior lay Pasargada, the ancient capital of Persia, and the burial-place of Kyros, in the neighbourhood of Murghâb, a place to the N. E. of Shiraz (30° 24′ N. 56° 29′ E.).

At the Sitakos they took on board a large supply
of provisions, which under orders from the king
had been collected expressly for the fleet. They
remained at this station one-and-twenty days in
all, occupied in repairing and kareening the ships,
which had been drawn on shore for the purpose.[75]

XXXIX. Weighing thence they came to an
inhabited district with a town called Hieratis,
after accomplishing a distance of 750 stadia.
They anchored in a canal which drew its waters
from a river and emptied into the sea, and was
called Heratemis.[79] Weighing next morning about
sunrise, and sailing by the shore, they reached a
winter torrent called the Padargos, where the
whole place was a peninsula, wherein were
many gardens and all kinds of trees that bear
fruit. The name of the place was Mesam-

---

[75] The Sitakos has been identified with the Kara Agach,
Mand, Mund or Kakee river, which has a course of 300
miles. Its source is near Kodiyan, which lies N. W. of
Shiraz. At a part of its course it is called the Kewar
River. The meaning of its name is *black wood*. In Pliny
it appears as the Sitioganus. *Sitakon* was probably the
name as Néarkhos heard it pronounced, as it frequently
happens that when a Greek writer comes upon a name
like an oblique case in Greek, he invents a nominative for it.
With regard to the form of the name in Pliny, 'g' is but a
phonetic change instead of 'k'. The 'i' is probably an
error in transcription for 't'. The Sitakos is probably the
Brisoana of Ptolemy, which can have no connexion with the
later-mentioned Brizana of our author. See *Report on the
Persian Gulf* by Colonel Ross, lately issued. Pliny states
that from the mouth of the Sitiogus an ascent could be
made to Pasargada, in seven days; but this is manifestly
an error.

[79] The changes which have taken place along the coast
have been so considerable that it is difficult to explain this
part of the narrative consistently with the now existing
state of things.

bria.[50] Weighing from Mesambria and running a course of about 200 stadia, they reach Taôkê on the river Granis, and there anchor. Inland from this lay a royal city of the Persians, distant from the mouths of the river about 200 stadia.[51] We learn from Nearkhos that on their way to Taôkê a stranded whale had been observed from the fleet, and that a party of the men having rowed alongside of it, measured it and brought back word that it had a length of 50 cubits. Its skin, they added, was clad with scales to a depth of about a cubit, and thickly clustered over with parasitic mussels, barnacles, and seaweed. The monster, it was also noticed, was attended by a great number of dolphins, larger than are ever seen in the Mediterranean. Weighing from Taôkê they proceeded to Rhogonis, a winter torrent. where they anchored in a safe harbour.[52] The course thither was one of 200 stadia. Weighing

---

[50] The peninsula, which is 10 miles in length and 3 in breadth, lies so low that at times of high tide it is all but submerged. The modern A b u-S h a h r or B u s h i r is situated on it.

[51] Nearkhos, it is probable, put into the mouth of the river now called by some the K i s h t, by others the Bosha-vir. A town exists in the neighbourhood called G r a or G r a n, which may have received its name from the Granis. The royal city (or rather palace), 200 stadia distant from this river, is mentioned by Strabo, xv. 3, 3, as being situate on the coast. Ptolemy does not mention the Granis. He makes Taôkê to be an inland town, and calls all the district in this part Taôkênê. Taokê may be the Touag mentioned by Idrisi, which is now represented by Konar Takhta near the Kisht.

[52] R h o g o n i s.—It is written Rhogomanis by Ammianus Marcellinus, who mentions it as one of the four largest rivers in Persia, the other three being the Vatrachitis, Brisoana, and Bagrada. It is the river at the mouth of which is Bender-Righ or Regh, which is considered now as in the days of Nearkhos to be a day's sail from Bushire.

· thence, and running 400 stadia, they arrived at
another winter torrent, called Brizana, where they
land and form an encampment. They had here
difficulty in anchoring because of shoals and
breakers and reefs that showed their heads above
the sea. They could therefore enter the roads
only when the tide was full; when it receded, the
ships were left high and dry.[83] They weighed
with the next flood tide, and came to anchor at the
mouth of a river called the Arosis, the greatest,
according to Nearkhos, of all the rivers that in
the course of his voyage fell into the outer ocean.[84]

XL. The Arosis marks the limit of the pos-
sessions of the Persians, and divides them from
the Susians. Above the Susians occurs an independent race called the Uxians, whom I have
described in my other work (Anab. VII. 15, 3) as
robbers. The length of the Persian coast is 4,400
stadia. Persis, according to general report, has
three different climates,[85] for that part of it which
lies along the Erythraean sea, is sandy and barren

[83] "The measures here are neglected in the Journal,
for we have only 800 stadia specified from Mesambria to
Brizana, and none from Brizana to the Arosis; but 800
stadia are short of 50 miles, while the real distance from
Mesambriă (Bushir) to the Arosis with the winding of the
coast is above 140. In these two points we cannot be
mistaken, and therefore, besides the omission of the interval
between Brizana and the Arosis, there must be some defect
in the Journal for which it is impossible now to account."
—Vincent. I. p. 405.

[84] Another form of the name of this river is the Aroătis.
It answers to the Zarotis of Pliny, who states that the
navigation at its mouth was difficult, except to those well
acquainted with it. It formed the boundary between
Persis and Susiana. The form Oroătis corresponds to the
Zend word aurwat 'swift.' It is now called the Tăb.

[85] On this point compare Strabo, bk. xv. 3, 1.

from the violence of the heat, while the part
which succeeds enjoys a delightful temperature,
for there the mountains stretch towards the pole
and the North wind, and the region is clothed
with verdure and has well-watered meadows, and
bears in profusion the vine and every fruit else
but the olive, while it blooms with gardens and
pleasure parks of all kinds, and is permeated with
crystal streams and abounds with lakes, and lake
and stream alike are the haunts of every variety
of water-fowl, and it is also a good country for
horses and other yoke cattle, being rich in pasture,
while it is throughout well-wooded and well-
stocked with game. The part, however, which
lies still further to the North is said to be bleak
and cold, and covered with snow, so that, as Nearkhos tells us, certain ambassadors from the
Euxine Sea, after a very brief journey, met Alexander marching forward to Persis, whereat
Alexander being greatly surprised, they explained
to him how very inconsiderable the distance was.[86]
I have already stated that the immediate neighbours to the Susians are the Uxians, just as the
Mardians, a race of robbers, are next neighbours
to the Persians, and the Kossaeans to the Medes.
All these tribes Alexander subdued, attacking
them in the winter time when their country
was, as they imagined, inaccessible. He then
founded cities to reclaim them from their wandering life, and encouraged them to till their lands
and devote themselves to agriculture. At the

---

[86] It has been conjectured that the text here is imperfect.
Schmieder opines that the story about the ambassadors is
a fiction.

same time he appointed magistrates armed with the terrors of the law to prevent them having recourse to violence in the settlement of their quarrels. On weighing from the Arosis the expedition coasted the shores of the Susians. The remainder of the voyage, Nearkhos says, he cannot describe with the same precision; he can but give the names of the stations and the length of the courses, for the coast was full of shoals and beset with breakers which spread far out to sea, and made the approach to land dangerous. The navigation thereafter was of course almost entirely restricted to the open sea. In mentioning their departure from the mouth of the river where they had encamped on the borders of Persis, he states that they took there on board a five days' supply of water, as the pilots had brought to their notice that none could be procured on the way.

XLI. A course of 500 stadia having been accomplished, their next anchorage was in an estuary, which swarmed with fish, called Kataderbis, at the entrance of which lay an island called Margastana.[87] They weighed at daybreak, the ships sailing out in single file through shoals. The direction of the shoal was indicated by stakes fixed both on the right and the left side, just as posts are erected as signals of danger in the passage between the island of Leukadia and Akarnania to prevent vessels grounding on the shoals. The shoals of Leukadia, however, are of firm sand, and

---

[87] The bay of Kataderbis is that which receives the streams of the Mensureh and Dorak; at its entrance lie two islands, Bunah and Deri, one of which is the Margastana of Arrian.

it is thus easy to float off vessels should they happen
to strand, but in this passage there is a deep mud
on both sides of such tenacity that if vessels once
touched the bottom, they could not by any ap-
pliances be got off; for, if they thrust poles into
the mud to propel the vessels, these found no
resistance or support, and the people who got over-
board to ease them off into navigable water found
no footing, but sunk in the mud higher than the
waist. The fleet proceeded 600 stadia, having
such difficulties of navigation to contend with,
and then came to an anchor, each crew remaining
in their own vessel, and taking their repast on
board. From this anchorage they weighed in the
night, sailing on in deep water till about the close
of the ensuing day, when, after completing a course
of 900 stadia, they dropped anchor at the mouth of
the Euphrates near a town in Babylonia called
Diridôtis—the emporium of the sea-borne trade in
frankincense and all the other fragrant produc-
tions of Arabia.[88] The distance from the mouth
of the Euphrates up stream to Babylon is, according to Nearkhos, 3,300 stadia.

XLII. Here intelligence having been received
that Alexander was marching towards Sousa, they
retraced their course from Diridôtis so as to join

---

[88] D i r i d ô t i s is called by other writers Terêdon, and
is said to have been founded by Nabukhodonosor. Mannert
places it on the island now called B u b i a n; Colonel
Chesney, however, fixes its position at J e b e l S a n â m,
a gigantic mound near the Pallacopas branch of the
Euphrates, considerably to the north of the embouchure of
the present Euphrates. Nearkhos had evidently passed
unawares the stream of the Tigris and sailed too far westward. Hence he had to retrace his course, as mentioned
in the next chapter.

him by sailing up the Pasitigris. They had now
Sousis on their left hand, and were coasting the
shores of a lake into which the Tigris empties
itself, a river, which flowing from Armenia past
Nineveh, a city once of yore great and flourishing, encloses between itself and the Euphrates the
tract of country which from its position between
the two rivers is called Mesopotamia. It is a distance of 600 stadia from the entrance into the lake
up to the river's mouth at Aginis, a village in
the province of Sousis, distant from the city of
Sousa 500 stadia. The length of the voyage along
the coast of the Sousians to the mouth of the
Pasitigris was 2,000 stadia.[59] Weighing from the

---

[59] This is the Eulæus, now called the K a r û n, one arm
of which united with the Tigris, while the other fell into
the sea by an independent mouth. It is the U l a i of the
prophet Daniel. *Pas* is said to be an old Persian word,
meaning *small*. By some writers the name P a s i t i g r i s
was applied to the united stream of the Tigris and
Euphrates, now called the S h a t-e l-A r a b. The courses of
the rivers and the conformation of the country in the parts
here have all undergone great changes, and hence the
identification of localities is a matter of difficulty and
uncertainty. The following extract from Strabo will
illustrate this part of the narrative:—
Polycletus says that the C h o a s p e s, and the E u l æ u s,
and the T i g r i s also enter a lake, and thence discharge
themselves into the sea; that on the side of the lake is a
mart, as the rivers do not receive the merchandize from the
sea, nor convey it down to the sea, on account of dams in
the river, purposely constructed; and that the goods are
transported by land, a distance of 800 stadia, to Susis:
according to others, the rivers which flow through Susis
discharge themselves by the intermediate canals of the
Euphrates into the single stream of the Tigris, which on
this account has at its mouth the name of Pasitigris.
According to Nearchus, the sea-coast of Susis is swampy,
and terminates at the river Euphrates; at its mouth is a
village which receives the merchandize from Arabia, for the
coast of Arabia approaches close to the mouths of the
Euphrates and the Pasitigris; the whole intermediate space

mouth of this river they sailed up its stream
through a fertile and populous country, and
having proceeded 150 stadia dropped anchor,
awaiting the return of certain messengers whom
Nearkhos had sent off to ascertain where the
king was. Nearkhos then presented sacrifices to
the gods their preservers, and celebrated games, and
full of gladness were the hearts of all that had taken
part in the expedition. The messengers having
returned with tidings that Alexander was approaching, the fleet resumed its voyage up the river,
and anchored near the bridge by which Alexander
intended to lead his army to Sousa. In that same
place the troops were reunited, when sacrifices
were offered by Alexander for the preservation of
his ships and his men, and games were celebrated.
Nearkhos, whenever he was seen among the
troops, was decorated by them with garlands and
pelted with flowers. There also both Nearkhos
and Leonnatos were crowned by Alexander with
golden diadems—Nearkhos for the safety of the
expedition by sea, and Leonnatos for the victory
which he had gained over the O r e i t a i and the
neighbouring barbarians. It was thus that the
expedition which had begun its voyage from the
mouths of the Indus was brought in safety to
Alexander.

occupied by a lake which receives the Tigris. On sailing
up the Pasitigris 150 stadia is a bridge of rafts leading to
Susa from Persia, and is distant from Susa 60 (600 ?) stadia ;
the Pasitigris is distant from the Oroätis about 2,000 stadia ;
the ascent through the lake to the mouth of the Tigris is
600 stadia ; near the mouth stands the Susian village
Aginis, distant from Susa 500 stadia ; the journey by water
from the mouth of the Euphrates up to Babylon, through
a well-inhabited tract of country, is a distance of more
than 3,000 stadia."—Book xv. 3, *Bohn's trans.*

XLIII. Now[90] the parts which lie to the right of the E r y t h r æ a n[91] S e a beyond the realms of Babylonia belong principally to A r a b i a, which extends in one direction as far as the sea that washes the shores of P h œ n i k i a and S y r i a n P a l e s- t i n e, while towards sunset it borders on the Egyp- tians in the direction of the M e d i t e r r a n e a n S e a. Egypt is penetrated by a gulf which ex- tends up from the great ocean, and as this ocean is connected with the E r y t h r æ a n S e a, this fact proves that a voyage could be made all the way from B a b y l o n to E g y p t by means of this gulf. But, owing to the heat and utter sterility of the coast, no one has ever made this voyage, except, it may be, some chance navigator. For the troops belonging to the army of K a m b y s ê s, which escaped from E g y p t, and reached S o u s a in safety, and the troops sent by P t o l e m y, the son of Lagos, to S e l e u k o s N i k a t ô r to B a b y l o n, traversed the Arabian isthmus in eight days altogether.[92] It was a waterless and sterile region, and they had to cross it mounted on swift camels carrying water, travelling only by night, the heat by day being so fierce that they could not expose themselves in the open air. So far are the parts lying beyond this region, which we have spoken of as an isthmus extending from the A r a b i a n G u l f to the E r y t h r æ a n S e a

---

[90] The 3rd part of the *Indika*, the purport of which is to prove that the southern parts of the world are uninhabit- able, begins with this chapter.

[91] Here and subsequently meaning the Persian Gulf.

[92] It is not known when or wherefore Ptolemy sent troops on this expedition.

from being inhabited, that even the parts which
run up further to the north are a desert of sand.
Moreover, men setting forth from the A r a b i a n
G u l f in E g y p t, after having sailed round the
greater part of A r a b i a to reach the sea which
washes the shores of P e r s i s and S o u s a, have
returned, after sailing as far along the coast of
Arabia as the water they had on board lasted
them, and no further. The exploring party again
which A l e x a n d e r sent from B a b y l o n with
instructions to sail as far as they could along
the right-hand coast of the E r y t h r æ a n S e a,
with a view to examine the regions lying in that
direction, discovered some islands lying in their
route, and touched also at certain points of the
mainland of A r a b i a. But as for that cape which
Nearkhos states to have been seen by the expedition projecting into the sea right opposite
to K a r m a n i a, there is no one who has been
able to double it and gain the other side. But if
the place could possibly be passed, either by
sea or by land, it seems to me that Alexander, being so inquisitive and enterprising, would
have proved that it could be passed in both
these ways. But again H a n n o the L i b y a n,
setting out from C a r t h a g e, sailed out into
the ocean beyond the Pillars of H e r c u l e s,
having L i b y a on his left hand, and the time
until his course was shaped towards the rising
sun was five-and-thirty days; but when he steered
southward he encountered many difficulties from
the want of water, from the scorching heat,
and from streams of fire that fell into the sea.
K y r ê n ê, no doubt, which is situated in a some-

what barren part of L i b y a, is verdant, possessed
of a genial climate, and well watered, has groves
and meadows, and yields abundantly all kinds of
useful animals and vegetable products. But this
is only the case up to the limits of the area within
which the fennel-plant can grow, while beyond
this area the interior of Kyrênê is but a desert of
sand.

So ends my narrative relating to A l e x a n d e r,
the son of Philip the Makedonian.

INDEX.

CHIEFLY GEOGRAPHICAL.

Abbreviations.—B. Bay, C. Cape, G. Gulf, Is. Island or Islands, M. Mountain, R. River.

Common names are printed in Italics. Many proper names which in the usual orthography begin with C, will be found under K.

d 2

Mr. J. W. McCrindle of Patna has given us a readable translation both of Schwanbeck's Megasthenês and of the first part of Arrian's *Indika*. Mr. McCrindle deserves the thanks of all who take an interest in Ancient India, and should he be able to fulfil his promise to translate " the entire series of classical works relating to India," he will give an impetus to the study of the early civilization of this country among native as well as European Scholars. His work is well printed, and, as far as we have been able to judge, carefully edited.—*The Madras Times*.

Mr. McCrindle, who has already published a portion of the translation of Arrian, reprints these valuable contributions to our scanty knowledge of ancient India. . . . . . An Introduction and notes add value to the translation, a value which happens to be very great in this case, and to centre in one long note on the identification of the old Palibothra or Pataliputra with the modern Patna.—*The Daily Review*.

Mr. McCrindle, who holds a very high position in the Education Department of the Indian Government, has collected into a volume some translations which he has lately contributed to the " Indian Antiquary" from Megasthenês and Arrian. . . . . . Strabo and Pliny thought fit to condemn the writings of Megasthenês as absolutely false, and incredible, although they were glad to copy into their own works much that he had written. We moderns, however, with our longer experience of travellers' tales, and of the vitality of fabulous statements, and practised in comparing accounts that vary, find much in these fragments that agrees with what we can reasonably conjecture of the past of India. . . . . . We may observe that many of the singularities of the human race which are depicted on the famous *Mappemonde* at Hereford are described by Megasthenês— Mr. McCrindle's volume ends with an excellent translation of the first part of Arrian's Indika. He is to be congratulated on having made a very useful contribution to the popular study of Indian Antiquities.—*Westminster Review*.

Other notices of a like favourable import have appeared in the " Englishman," the " Scotsman," the " Saturday Review," and several Indian vernacular publications.

12

Lightning Source UK Ltd.
Milton Keynes UK
UKOW01f1033090218
317570UK00004B/491/P